50 Shades of Gravy

Fifty Seductively Smutty Recipes

For Cooks With Their Minds In The Gutter

by

Dr. Maddog

(a.k.a. Mark Donnelly, Ph.D.)

All rights reserved. Copyright © 2014 by Dr. Mark D. Donnelly

Text and design by Mark D. Donnelly, Ph.D.

This book contains photographs by Dr. Mark Donnelly, Laura Donnelly, and stock photography from 123rf.com.

www.rpsspublishing.com

All rights reserved. No part of this publication may be reproduced or distributed in any form or by any means, or stored in a database or retrieval system, without the prior written permission of the publisher.
publisher@rockpapersafetyscissors.com

ISBN 978-0-9908997-2-3

Printed in the United States of America

10 9 8 7 6 5 4 3 2 1

Sexy, nutrition-free recipes

to help you make

good use of your

lingerie and stretch pants

Let's talk dirty in the kitchen

The intersection of food and sex is so profound that it should be no surprise that the language of these two primal passions dovetail so closely. Feeding has always been closely linked with courtship ever since Marc Antony first fed Cleopatra grapes.

In nature, the short distance between consumption and consummation is not without its dangers. The female praying mantis devours the male after mating. Once his job is completed he instantly becomes a meal for the now expectant mother.

Fortunately, human males have learned from this teachable tidbit. They've figured out that it is far more sustainable to their lifespan to quell their dates appetite by taking them out for dinner.

"One cannot think well, love well, sleep well, if one has not dined well."
- Virginia Woolf

Women used to be taught that one way to a man's heart is through his stomach.

Some men eat bull testicles and oysters to increase sexual potency.

And chocolates, long been thought to be an aphrodisiac are a traditional gift for Valentine's Day. In fact, in the 1600s chocolate was considered such a powerful passion potion that religious leaders banned its consumption for monks and nuns. Emperor Montezuma is said to have drunk 50 cups of chocolate a day in order to keep up with his more than 200 wives.

Food is seductive. Food is sexy. Food is fun. It only makes sense that preparing food should also be seductive, sexy, and fun!

Fifty Shades of Gravy is a satirical look at food and the sexual vocabulary it brings to the table, with fifty terrific recipes that help us to laugh at ourselves. It's an examination of the head-on collision of sexual slang and food, combined with fourth-grade humor, and enough meaningless trivia to make you a complete bore on a first date.

This book is merely the illusion of being obscene. Other than the word chicken, this book has no foul language, and the photographs are no more pornographic than your average department store catalog. The only thing vulgar about these recipes is the frame of mind you bring with you. In the true spirit of Lenny Bruce, this book is just a way to laugh at the words that sometimes divide us.

Make this book an excuse to be bold, creative, and adventurous. And above all, use this book to have fun as you cook. So here are fifty ways to get busy in the kitchen. Clothing optional.

Let's get busy in the kitchen!

Introduction   4

Rude Awakenings
9

Nooners
23

Meat in Heat
37

Cock
51

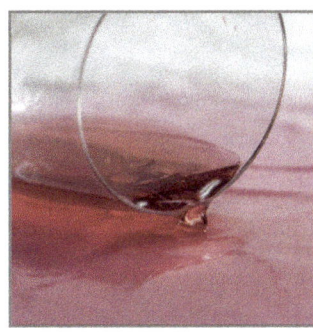

Love Potions
107

Smells Like Fish
67

Quickies
117

Lingerie Stretchers
79

Size Matters 128

Index 129

Foreplay
95

The creepy old guy who writes this stuff
132

Rude Awakenings

Nurishment served between last call and lunch

Mini Egg Frittatas with Turkey, Spinach, and Cheese

•

French Toast Breakfast Sandwich with Applewood Bacon

•

The Kama Sutra of Makin' Bacon

•

Eggs Benedict with Avocado Hollandaise

•

Pigs in a Blanket

Getting Laid
(Mini-Egg Frittatas with Panchetta, Spinach, and Cheese)

Eggs get laid on average of once a day, always with the lights on, and then they get graded for it.

Now that's pressure.

Preheat oven to 350°F.
Prepare six muffin tin cups with cooking spray.

Brown Panchetta in a medium skillet. Set aside.

In a large mixing bowl, whisk eggs, egg whites and milk. Season with salt, pepper, and thyme and add the chopped spinach and shallots.

Pour egg mixture evenly into the muffin cups. Equally distribute the Panchetta and cheese between each cup.

Bake for 20 minutes, or until firm in the center. Serve warm.

6 ounces Panchetta, diced

2 whole eggs

5 egg whites

1/4 cup milk

Salt and pepper

1/4 teaspoon thyme

1/4 cup fresh spinach, chopped

1 shallot, minced

1/4 cup Havarti cheese, shredded

Morning Wood
(French Toast Breakfast Sandwich with Applewood Bacon)

For the French Toast:

2 eggs, beaten

1/4 cup Half and Half

4 slices bread

For the Sandwich:

4 slices Applewood bacon

2 eggs

1/2 cup maple syrup

Morningwood Condominiums was the fictional residence of Peter Gibbons in the 1999 comedy "Office Space."

Unfortunately, the film made no reference to what they ate there for breakfast.

Place bacon in a large, deep skillet. Cook over medium high heat until it browns evenly to desired crispness. Drain and set aside. Reserve 1 tablespoon of bacon grease in pan and fry remaining two eggs.

Dip bread slices in beaten eggs. Cook bread in skillet until browned on both sides. Set aside.

Build a sandwich layering French toast, a fried egg, two slices of bacon, and cover with French toast. Serve warm with syrup.

The Kama Sutra of Makin' Bacon

Diamond, chocolates, and flowers move over.

When it's time to show the ultimate expression of love, say it on a plate. Or, as Oscar Mayer's promotional bacon website (http://www.sayitwithbacon.com) so poetically waxes,
I love you like I love this bacon, except there is nothing about this bacon I'd like to change.

I will love you until the day you take the last strip of bacon.

Skillet
A cast-iron skillet is necessary for this classic method of cooking bacon. The older, the blacker the skillet the better. There are those who will say that any kind of skillet will do. Bullpucky.

Lay the strips of bacon in a cold skillet. Turn on a medium-low flame. Flip the bacon when it begins to curl. Continue turning the bacon to brown evenly. Remove when cooked to the desired crispness and drain on a paper towel. Save the bacon grease for future frying.

Microwave
Perfect for those times when you just want a few slices of bacon.
Line a microwave-safe dish with 2-4 layers of paper towels to soak up all the grease from the bacon.

Place up to 8 slices of bacon on the paper towels. Don't overlap the slices.

Cover with 2 more sheets of paper towel on top.

Heat in the microwave on high power for 1 minute per slice. The bacon will continue to cook a little more and become crisper once you remove it from the microwave. Transfer the bacon to a plate because it tends to stick to the paper towels. Be very careful. The bacon and plate will be super hot, like models from the 20s.

The Kama Sutra of Makin' Bacon - cont.

Oven
For cooking bacon in bulk.

Preheat the oven to 400°F. Prepare a foil-lined baking sheet.

Bake for 15 minutes, slightly longer for thicker bacon. Remove when cooked to the desired crispness and drain on a paper towel.

Grill it
Prepare grill with high heat on one side and no flame on the other.

Place the strips of bacon onto the cool side of the grill. The bacon fat will still drip down into the grill, but since there are no flames underneath, flare-ups will be minimal. Make sure the slices do not touch.

Cook the bacon until the bottom has begun to get crisp and golden, then flip and repeat. Total cooking time will be between 5-7 minutes. When the bacon is at the desired crispness, remove it from the grill and place it onto a plate lined with several layers of paper towels.

Under the Hood
Everything is better with bacon - including road trips.

Discovering your manifold destiny requires mass quantities of aluminum foil. Use a sheet of foil large enough to comfortably cover your bacon laid in a single layer, and then twisting the foil on top making it look like a giant Hershey's kiss. Repeat twice more so that you have a triple layer of well-sealed foil.

With the car turned off, place your package of hog heaven on top of the engine block. Be sure not to disturb any wires or the accelerator linkage that connects the gas pedal to the carburetor or fuel-injection system.

After a few hours of driving, remove the package and allow to cool before attempting to open.

Crack of Dawn
(Eggs Benedict with Avocado Hollandaise)

For the Avocado Hollandaise Sauce:

1 medium Hass avocado

1/4 cup lemon juice (1 lemon)

Salt to taste

1 teaspoon Extra Virgin Olive Oil

For the Egg Benedict:

1 teaspoon vinegar

4 eggs

8 slices of Prosciutto

2 Brioche rolls, lightly toasted

For the Plumber:

1 can of Spackle *

*Don't lick the spoon.

When a plumber bends over and advertises his cheek cleavage, it's simply his way of letting you know that he accepts loose change and major credit cards.

Swipe away.

In a food processor or blender, puree the avocado, lemon juice, extra virgin olive oil, and salt until smooth.

Add vinegar to 2 quarts water in a wide 3-quart heavy saucepan and bring to a simmer.

In a small bowl, break 1 egg and gently lower it into the water. Repeat with the remaining eggs, and poach until whites are firm and yolks are still runny, approximately 2 to 3 minutes. Transfer eggs to paper towels using a slotted spoon.

Place 4 slices of Prosciutto on each Brioche roll, top with the poached eggs, and Hollandaise.

Servings: 2 servings

Going Commando
(Pigs in a Blanket)

Around the world, what we refer to as Pigs in a Blanket is known by many names. In Scotland they're called Kilted Sausages, and are traditionally served for Christmas dinner.

Kilts, which are a part of Scottish military uniform, are traditionally worn without undergarments. This has lead to the slang expressions for not wearing underwear as "Go Regimental" or with a post-Viet Nam twist, "Going Commando."

In the true spirit of Kilted Sausages, to avoid creating a panty line, this free-balling recipe does not call for either boxers or tighty-whiteys.

Preheat the oven to 375°F, and position a rack in the center.

Separate the dinner roll dough into triangles and brush the top edges with the egg wash. Lay a half slice of bacon on the dough and wrap both around each sausage. Press the edges to seal. Place on ungreased cookie sheet.

Bake for 12 to 15 minutes or until golden brown. Turn out onto a paper towel-lined rack to cool.

- 1 can (8 ounce) Pillsbury™ crescent dinner rolls
- 1 large egg yolk mixed with 1 tablespoon of water
- 2 slices of Bacon, cut in half
- 4 (3 ounce) andouille sausages

Nooners

Eating in Lieu of Sex

Variations of Hot Dogs Across the Country
•
Feta Fries
•
Spicy Beef Kabob
•
Tomato and Hearts of Palm Salad
•
Salami Sandwich

Doggy-Style

1 Uncircumcised Hot Dog
1 Hot Dog roll
Condiments of your choice

When it comes to eating tube steaks, people in different cities get it on in different ways.

New York City
Typically sold from the sidewalk cart, hot dogs in the Big Apple are adorned with little more than brown mustard and onions stewed in tomato paste.

Kansas City
Dorothy clicks her ruby heels to go home to a fusion of the traditional ballpark frank, and the Reuben sandwich. All stacked high with corned beef and Swiss; these all-beef dogs are typically topped with melted cheese, caraway, sauerkraut, and Thousand Island dressing.

New Jersey
New Jersey is known for its deep-fried hot dogs that burst open, splitting their outer casing. Affectionately called "Rippers," these heart attacks on a bun are often served with mustard, relish, onions, carrots and cabbage.

Atlanta
Atlantan's love to order their savory dogs blanketed with coleslaw or "dragged through the garden."

Chicago
Iconic dogs from the Windy City come buried with an array of toppings, including fresh tomatoes, pickle spears, hot peppers, relish, and onion. Don't even think about requesting ketchup.

Montréal
Whether you get steamed "steamies," or griddle fried "toasties," the hockey players and other residents of Montréal like their dogs topped with coleslaw, onion, mustard, relish, and occasionally paprika or chili powder.

Buffalo
Long before Buffalo invented its famous wings, the legendary Ted's Hot Dogs was charcoal broiling over real hardwood. Available in both a regular, foot-long size, they come dressed with ketchup, mustard, onion, relish, and a special hot sauce.

On Top, Greek-Style
(Feta Fries)

In Greek-style in the late classical period (400-300 B.C.) there was increased emphasis on the expression of emotion in art. Sculptural works attributed to Praxiteles are characterized by elegance of proportion and graceful beauty.

Powerful emotional effects are typical of the sculpture in the style of Scopas, as he bent over backwards to create a new feeling of individualization and three-dimensional movement.

Preheat oven to 400°F.

Peel and rinse the potatoes. Cut them into sticks about 1/8-inch thick.

In a large mixing bowl, add potatoes, olive oil, garlic powder, and oregano and toss until completely coated.

Make an even layer of coated potatoes on a baking sheet.

Bake for 25 minutes.

Remove sheet from the oven and flip fries over. Place the sheet back in oven and bake for another 10 minutes or until golden brown.

Place on a serving dish and liberally sprinkle with feta.

Serves: 4-6. Togas optional.

5 Russet potatoes

1/4 cup olive oil

1 teaspoon garlic powder

1 teaspoon oregano

1/2 teaspoon lemon juice

1/4 cup Feta cheese

1 tablespoon parsley

Salt and pepper to taste

Hot Meat Dip Stick
(Spicy Beef Kabob)

The Urban Dictionary defines dip stick as one who's brain compacity is less than a long thin piece of metal used to check oil levels.

Example: This dip stick's cranium is down a quart.

Preheat the grill to medium-high heat.

In a large, sealable plastic bag, combine the garlic, paprika, turmeric, cumin, salt, pepper, red wine vinegar, and olive oil.

Place the beef cubes in the bag and allow to marinate in the refrigerator for 2 to 4 hours.

Thread the meat onto the skewers leaving a space between the pieces. Place on the grill turning 1/4 rotation every 2 to 3 minutes, or until the meat is cooked throughout.

Allow to rest for 2 to 3 minutes before serving.

2 pounds boneless beef sirloin, cut into 1 1/2 to 1 3/4-inch cubes
3 cloves garlic, minced
2 teaspoons paprika
1/2 teaspoon ground turmeric
1 teaspoon ground cumin
1 teaspoon kosher salt
1/2 teaspoon black pepper
1/3 cup red wine vinegar
1/2 cup olive oil

Special equipment:
Metal or bamboo skewers

Rosie O'Palm
(Tomato and Hearts of Palm Salad)

3 cups cherry tomatoes

1-15 ounce can hearts of palm, drained and sliced in 1/4 inch rings

1/4 cup red onion, thinly sliced

1/4 cup Italian parsley, chopped

1/4 cup fresh basil, chopped

6 ounces fresh mozzerella, sliced

1/2 cup extra-virgin olive oil

1-1/2 tablespoons red vinegar

1 teaspoon sugar

1 teaspoon salt

1/2 teaspoon pepper

"I've got me a date with sweet Rosie O'Palm,
That handy little Irish girl who never says no."
-Unknown

Combine tomatoes, hearts of palm, red onion, parsley, basil, and fresh mozzerella slices in a large bowl.

In a small bowl, whisk together olive oil, vinegar, sugar, and salt and pepper until sugar is dissolved. Pour vinaigrette over tomato mixture and stir to coat.

Cover and refrigerate for at least one hour.

Serve at room temperature.

Hide the Salami
(Salami Sandwich)

Hide the salami is a popular game played during halftime at the submarine races.

Cut the ciabatta loaf lengthwise. Pour the Italian dressing on the top slice and set aside.

Build layers of the Prosciutto, Capicola, Soppressata, and Provolone on the bottom slice of the bread. Scatter a layer of roasted red peppers on top of the meats and cover with the top half of the ciabatta.

Cut crosswise into 6 sandwiches.

Serve as soon as you can find it.

1 large Ciabatta loaf
1/2 cup Italian dressing
1 cup roasted red peppers
6 ounces Prosciutto, thinly sliced
6 ounces hot Capicola, thinly sliced
6 ounces Soppressata, thinly sliced
8 ounces Provolone, thinly sliced

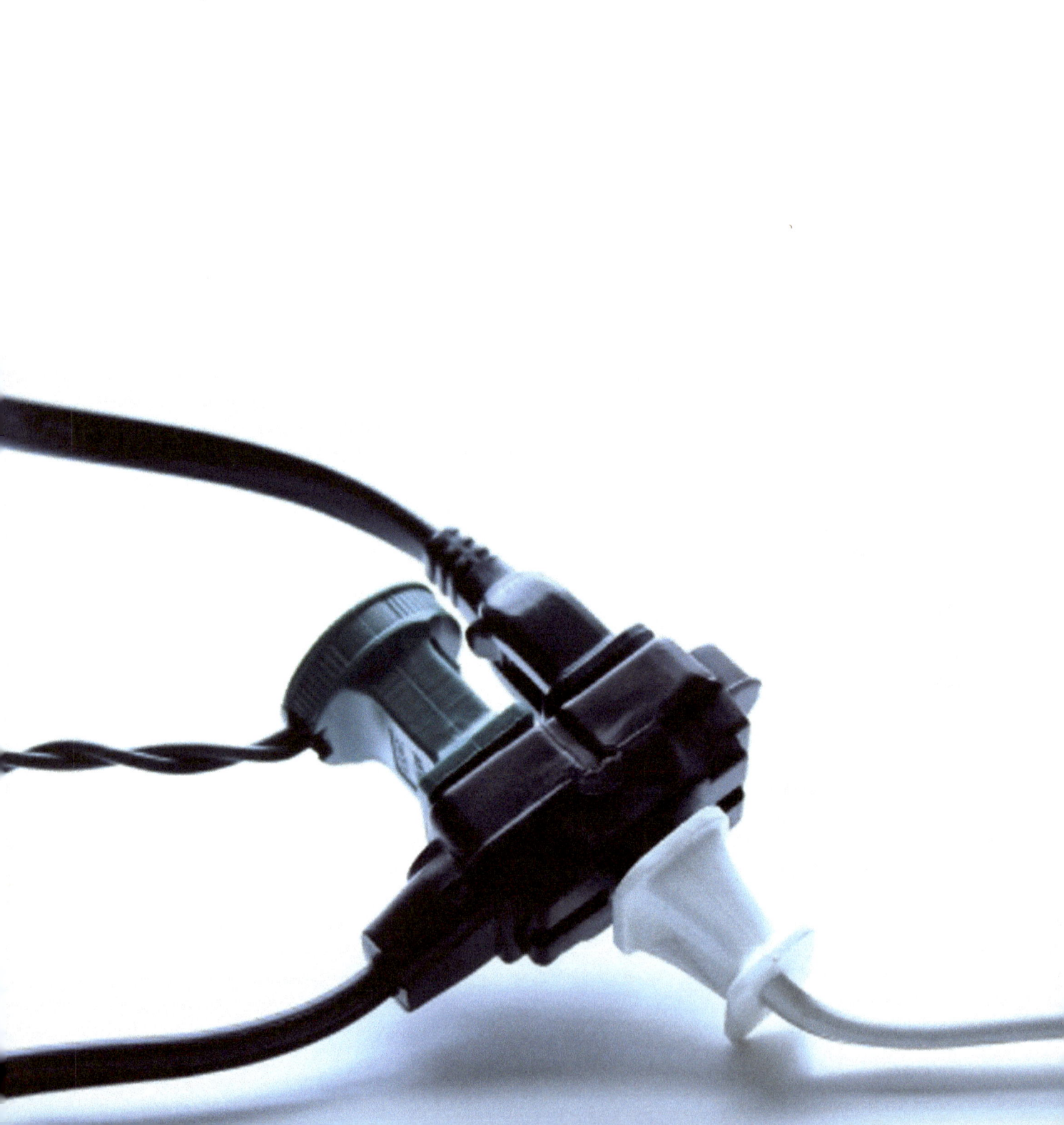

Ménage à Trois
(Cinncinatti Three-Way Chili)

2 tablespoons olive oil

5 cloves garlic, finely chopped

2 medium yellow onions, finely chopped

1-1/2 pounds ground beef

2 tablespoons chili powder

1-1/2 teaspoons ground cinnamon

1/2 teaspoon ground allspice

1/2 teaspoon ground cloves

1/2 teaspoons ground cumin

1 teaspoon dried oregano

1/2 teaspoon ground nutmeg

1/2 teaspoon celery seed

1 dried bay leaf

Salt and black pepper to taste

2 cups tomato sauce

1 tablespoon unsweetened cocoa powder

3/4 pound dried spaghetti

4 cups finely grated cheddar cheese

Ménage à Trois is French for "household of three."

Ménage à Deux is Ménage à Trois for those who passed French, but failed math.

In an oiled large skillet, saute garlic and onions until lightly browned. Add beef, chili powder, cinnamon, allspice, cloves, cumin, oregano, nutmeg, celery seed, bay leaf, and salt and pepper. Stir occasionally, until well browned. Spoon out extra fat.

Add tomato sauce, cocoa powder, and 1 cup water and bring to a boil. Reduce heat and cook uncovered for 20 minutes.

Add spaghetti to a large pot of boiling, salted water. Cook until al dente and drain. Divide spaghetti evenly between 3 large bowls. Top with chili and cheese. Serve hot.

Serves 3

Cock

A rooster by any other name would not have gotten your attention

Spinach and Artichoke Stuffed Chicken with Corn Flake Crust

•

Turkey Tetrazzini

•

Stuffed Chicken Leg with Ricotta and Panchetta Stuffing

•

Chicken Breasts Stuffed with Chorizo Sausage

•

Baked Chicken Tenders with Rosemary and Parmesan

•

Chicken on the Throne

Choke Your Chicken
(Spinach and Artichoke Stuffed Chicken with Corn Flake Crust)

6 boneless chicken breasts

Stuffing:

1 pound spinach

8 ounces artichoke hearts, drained and chopped

1/2 cup Asiago cheese, grated

1/4 teaspoon garlic, minced

1 cup chopped white onion

1 teaspoon fresh parsley leaves

Salt and pepper

Coating Mixture:

1 cup Corn Flakes, crushed

Parmesan cheese, grated

1 egg, beaten

1 teaspoon honey

1 teaspoon dijon mustard

1/4 teaspoon lemon juice

This is a very conflicted recipe.

On the one hand, ancient Greeks and Romans considered artichokes an aphrodisiac.

On the other hand, this dish is coated with Corn Flakes, a health food originally conceived by John Harvey Kellogg to suppress masturbation, or as he refered to it, the abomination of self-pollution. One of his many theories was that one could curb one's sexual appetite by eating bland foods.

Pre-heat oven to 375°F.

Prepare a 13 x 9-inch glass baking dish with cooking spray.

In medium bowl, microwave spinach approximately 2-3 minutes until wilted. Spank spinach dry with paper towels. Mix in artichokes, garlic, onion, parsley, and Asiago cheese.

Place each chicken breast smooth side down between pieces of plastic wrap, and beat your meat with a rolling pin until about 1/8 inch thick. Sprinkle with salt and pepper. Place equal portions of the spinach artichoke mixture on center of each flattened chicken breast. Fold in sides and roll up. Secure with a toothpick.

On shallow plate, mix Corn Flake crumbs and Parmesan cheese. In a small bowl add all of the coating mixture liquid ingredients. Dip chicken in coating mixture, then roll in Corn Flakes.

Bake 30 to 35 minutes, turning once, until light golden brown.

Peeping Tom
(Leftover Turkey Tetrazzini)

According to legend, Lady Godiva, wife of Leofric, Earl of Mercia, rode naked through Coventry to try and lower the heavy taxes imposed by her husband. A tailor named Tom Godgifu was the only person to observe her as she rode by, everyone else having shuttered their windows as they had been asked. Tom immediately opened a popular strip club capitalizing on the rest of the town who "weren't watching."

Preheat oven to 375°F.

In a large heavy saucepan over moderate heat, stir in 6 tablespoons of butter and the flour until melted. Stir in milk, broth, and the wine, bringing the mixture to a boil. Simmer the sauce for 5 minutes.

In a large pot of salted boiling water, cook the egg noodles until they are al dente. Drain it well.

In a large bowl combine the sauce, egg noodles, turkey, 1/3 cup of the Parmesan, and salt and pepper to taste. Transfer the mixture to a buttered shallow 3-quart casserole.

In a small bowl combine Panko bread crumbs with the remaining 1/3 cup Parmesan. Distribute the mixture evenly over the casserole and dot the top with the remaining 2 tablespoons butter.

Bake for 30 to 40 minutes, or until it is bubbling and the top is golden.

Serves: 4-6

1 stick of butter

1/4 cup all-purpose flour

1 3/4 cups milk

2 cups chicken broth

1/4 cup dry white wine

10 ounces large egg noodles

3 cups cooked turkey, coarsely chopped

2/3 cup Parmesan, grated

Salt and pepper

1/3 cup Panko bread crumbs

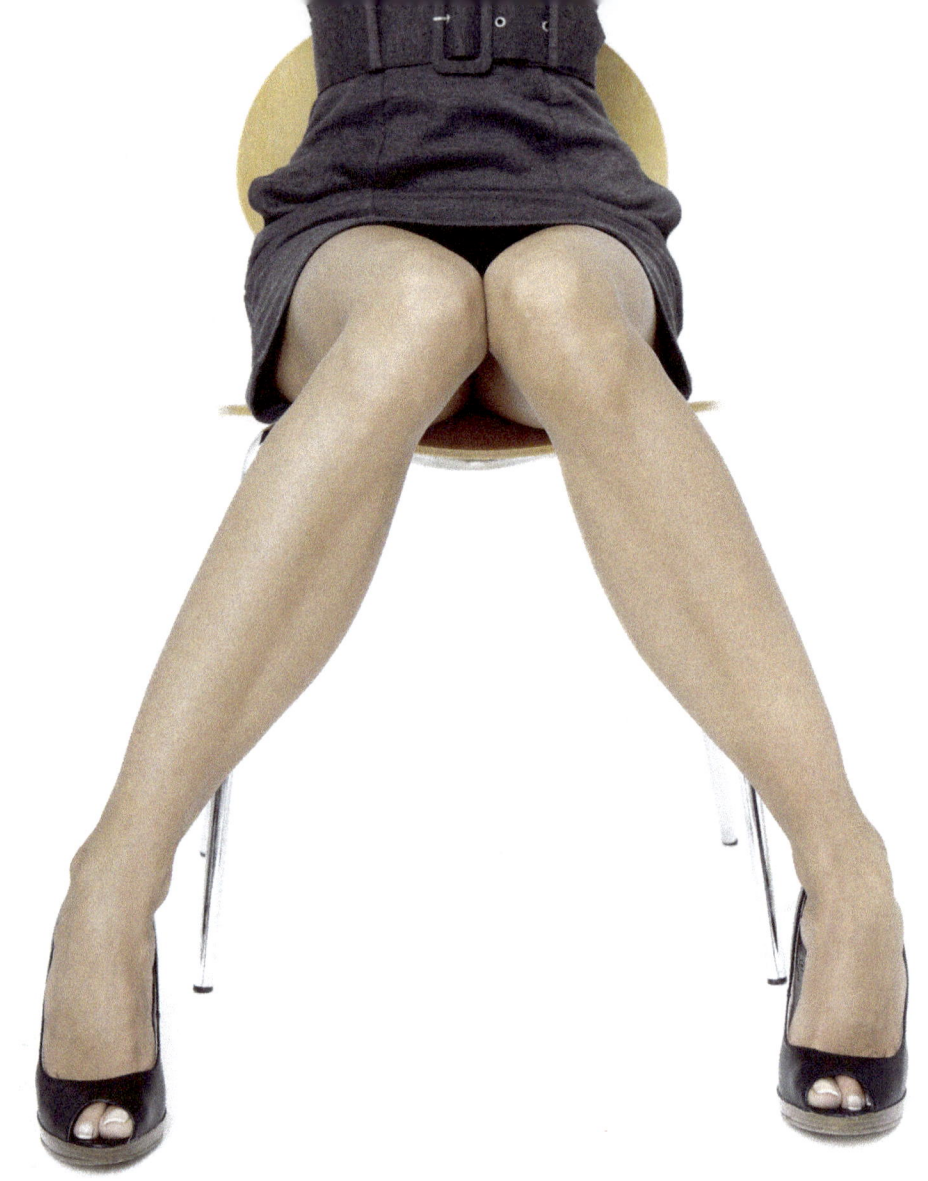

Legs Spread Wide Open and Stuffed
(Stuffed Chicken Leg with Ricotta and Panchetta Stuffing)

6 chicken legs with thighs attached

1/2 ounce butter, melted

1/2 cup Panchetta, cut in small cubes

1 tablespoon vegetable oil

2 tablespoons shallots, chopped

1/2 green pepper, coarsely chopped

Pinch of sage

1 clove garlic, crushed

8 ounces ricotta cheese

1 egg, beaten

2 tablespoons parmesan cheese, grated

1 cup fresh breadcrumbs

1/4 cup fresh parsley, chopped

There once was a girl who stood on her right leg, and then on her left leg. Between the two, she made a living.

I first heard this stale Burlesque joke when I was about seven. I didn't understand it, but all the adults in the room were laughing so I knew it somehow must be funny.

One day in my third-grade class, we all took turns telling jokes. I was relieved to know that the rest of the kids in the class didn't understand that joke either. And fortunately I had a very understanding principal.

Preheat oven to 350°F.

Fry the Panchetta in a dry pan until crisp. Remove and set aside. In the same pan, heat the oil and cook the green peppers, shallots and garlic until soft.

In a large bowl, lightly mix the ricotta, egg, Parmesan, breadcrumbs, sage, Panchetta, shallots, green pepper, and garlic.

Slice the thigh portion of the leg half way down and remove the thigh bone. Over stuff the cavity now created and close the flap over the stuffing.

Place the chicken in a lightly oiled, shallow roasting pan. Brush chicken with the melted butter. Roast for 40 minutes, or until the chicken is cooked thoroughly.

Remove from oven and allow to sit for 5 minutes before serving.

Breast Implants
(Chicken Breasts Stuffed with Chorizo Sausage)

Not satisfied with just using Kleenex, a 42-year-old woman in Stockholm, Sweden tried to smuggle 75 live baby snakes onto a plane by hiding them in her bra. She also reportedly had six lizards under her shirt, apparently with the dreams of starting a reptile farm.

Officials nabbed her after seeing her repeatedly scratch her chest.

Preheat oven to 400°F.

With a paring knife, cut a pocket into each of the chicken breasts. Stuff the pockets with chorizo and season with salt and freshly ground pepper.

In a saute pan over medium-high heat add olive oil and butter. Once the oil begins to smoke, sear the chicken breasts on all sides. Transfer the pan to the oven for 25 minutes to finish cooking.

- 4 boneless and skin-on chicken breasts
- 1/2 pound Mexican Chorizo (uncured and removed from casing)
- Salt and Pepper
- 3 tablespoons olive oil
- 3 tablespoons Butter

Giving the Finger
(Baked Chicken Tenders with Rosemary and Parmesan)

1 pound boneless, skinless chicken breasts, thinly cut

1 cup all-purpose flour

2 large eggs, whisked

1-1/2 cup Panko bread crumbs

1/2 cup Parmigiano-Reggiano, grated

1 teaspoon dried rosemary, ground

1 teaspoon kosher salt

1/2 teaspoon black pepper

Bleu cheese for dipping.

According to Wikipedia, so you know it has to be right, the first documented appearance of someone flipping the bird in the United States was in 1886. Old Hoss Radbourn, a baseball pitcher for the Boston Beaneaters, was photographed flashing it to a member of the rival New York Giants.

Preheat oven to 375°F.

This recipe requires three mixing bowls. One with the flour, one with the whisked eggs, and one with the panko mixed with Parmigiano-Reggiano, rosemary, salt and pepper.

Coat each piece of chicken in the flour, then dip in the egg mixture, and finally coated in the panko.

Place on a sheet pan, and bake for 20-30 minutes or until golden brown and cooked through.

Serve with bleu cheese or your favorite dipping sauce.

Serves 2-4

Fully-Erect Bird
(Chicken on the Throne)

2 (3-4 pound) fryer chickens

1 teaspoon salt

1 teaspoon cracked black pepper

2 small onions

1 whole lemon, cut in half

2 cloves garlic, crushed

2 cups of chardonnay or other white wine

Special Equipment:

2- 1 pint Mason jars

We often hear that good posture is essential for good health. Tell that to this chicken.

On a two burner grill preheat one side to 400°F, and the second burner off.

Discard the giblets and neck, and thoroughly rinse the chicken inside and out. Pat dry with paper towels.

Coat the chicken with olive oil and liberally season inside and out with salt and pepper. Set aside.

Add 1 half lemon and crushed garlic to each Mason jar. Fill the jars 2/3 of the way up with white wine.

Stuff a small onion in the chicken's neck cavity to prevent steam from escaping, Grabbing a chicken leg in each hand, push the lower bird cavity over the Mason jar until it is inside the body cavity.

Grill chicken on the non-flame side of the grate and cook with the grill cover on until chicken is golden brown, the juices run clear, and the internal temperature at the thigh is 180°F - approximately 1 hour to 1 1/2 hours.

Remove from the grill and allow to rest for 10 minutes before carving.

Serves: 4-6

Meat in Heat

There's nothing better than a well-hung sausage

Meatballs With Pasta in Broth

•

Twice-Baked Potato with Sloppy Joe Stuffing

•

Strip Steak Sandwich

•

Pulled Pork

•

Sausages and Mashed Potatoes in Gravy

•

Briciole

•

Grilled Mojo-Marinated Skirt Steak

Hairy Balls
(Meatballs With Pasta in Broth)

As any geek worth their pocket calculator will tell you, the "Hairy Ball" theorem of algebraic topology states that there is no non-vanishing continuous tangent vector field on even dimensional n-spheres.

The non-geek translation is that given a ball with hairs all over it, it is impossible to comb the hairs continuously and have all the hairs lay flat. Mathematically, some hair must be sticking straight up!

This was profoundly stated in 1912 by philosopher and mathematician Luitzen Egbertus Jan Brouwer as "you can't comb the hair on a coconut without creating a cowlick."

In a large bowl, thoroughly combine meats, bread crumbs, oregano, Parmigiano-Reggiano, black pepper, and garlic powder. Mix well and divide equally into 15 balls.

Carefully pierce meatballs with uncooked spaghetti noodles all the way through from all directions so that the final product looks similar to a porcupine.

In a large pot, boil the chicken stock. Add salt and pepper and lower heat to medium. Carefully drop the meatballs into the broth using a slotted spoon. Simmer until the spaghetti is soft and the meatballs are cooked.

Ladle into bowls and garnish with parsley

Meatballs:
8 ounces ground beef chuck
8 ounces ground veal
8 ounces ground pork
1/2 cup dry bread crumbs
1 teaspoon dried oregano
2 tablespoons Parmigiano-Reggiano, grated
1/4 teaspoon ground black pepper
1/8 teaspoon garlic powder
1/4 pound spaghetti, broken into 3-4 inch pieces

Broth:
4 quarts chicken stock
Salt and pepper to taste
Flat leaf parsley to garnish

Sloppy Seconds
(Twice-Baked Potato with Sloppy Joe Stuffing)

6 medium baking potatoes

1 pound lean ground beef

1/2 cup chopped onion

1/2 cup chopped green pepper

3 cloves garlic, minced

Salt and pepper

1 tablespoon flour

1 cup beef broth

1 tablespoon Worcestershire sauce

1/2 cup tomato paste

1/4 cup barbecue sauce

3/4 cup Cheddar cheese, shredded

Topping:

6 tablespoons sour cream

1/3 cup green onions, sliced

The second is the base unit of time. Until 1960, the second was defined as 1/86,400 of a mean solar day.

Since it has been determined that the mean solar day is slowly but measurably lengthening, the second is now defined to be the duration of 9,192,631,770 periods of the radiation corresponding to the transition between the two hyperfine levels of the ground state of the caesium 133 atom.

So, thanks to some wonky scientist, there will no longer be sloppy seconds.

Preheat oven to 425°F.

Thoroughly scrub the potatoes. Prick them with a fork in several places and wrap in foil. Bake for about an hour or until cooked through.

In a skillet, over medium high heat, sauté ground beef, onion, pepper and garlic. Cook, stirring occasionally until meat is completely browned. Drain grease. Stir in beef broth, Worcestershire sauce, tomato paste, barbecue sauce, and flour. Cook uncovered for about 20 minutes. Season to taste with salt and pepper.

Cut slit in top of each potato and carefully scoop out half of the inside. Combine removed potato with meat. Top each potato with 1/2 cup meat mixture, 2 tablespoons cheese. Return to oven for 1 minute to melt the cheese.

Top each potato with 1 tablespoon of sour cream and sprinkle with green onions.

Strip Club
(Strip Steak Sandwich)

In dancing around the kitchen as I cook, I've been told that I do equally as well with or without a pole.

In other words, not very well.

Preheat the grill on high for direct grilling.

Place steak on the grill with tongs (never a fork). For nice grill marks rotate the steak 90 degrees after about 2 minutes.

After four total minutes on the grill, flip the steak. After another 2 minutes, rotate the steak another 90 degrees for perfect grill marks.

After 8 total minutes, take the steaks off the grill and let them rest for at least 5 minutes before serving.

Cut strip steak into two equal pieces. On the bottom of each roll place 1 piece of steak, a slice of tomato, and a slice of onion. Top with steak sauce and cover with top of roll.

Now, undress your sandwich, one slow bite at a time.

---

1 inch thick New York Strip steak at room temperature

2 crusty rolls, split

2 slices tomato

2 slices onion

A1 Steak Sauce

Pulling Your Pork

1 cup molasses

1/2 cup cider vinegar

1/2 cup ketchup

1/2 cup yellow mustard

1 teaspoon paprika

1 teaspoon salt

1 teaspoon black pepper

1/2 teaspoon cayenne pepper

1/2 teaspoon garlic powder

3 to 3 ½ pound pork shoulder

According to the website potbellypigs.com, it is not uncommon to include pigs as part of their families. Many actually allow them to share their bed. They maintain that a porcine sleeping partner is not only warm and cuddly, but they don't wiggle, squirm, or hog the bed. They do however smack their lips and chew with their mouths open.

In a medium size mixing bowl, mix together all of the ingredients except the pork shoulder.

Place the pork shoulder in a slow cooker. Top it with sauce mixture.

Set the slow cooker on low and cook for 7 to 8 hours, flipping the roast 2 or 3 times during the cooking process.

Cook until the meat is fall off the bone tender.

Remove the meat from the pot and shred completely.

Feed this to the pig you share a bed with.

Sputtering Bangers with White Sauce
(Sausages and Mashed Potatoes in Gravy)

2 pounds bangers or thick pork sausages

1 tablespoon vegetable oil

For the mash:

2 lb. Russet potatoes, peeled and cut into medium sized chunks.

Sea salt

1/3 cup milk

2 tablespoons butter

Salt and pepper, to taste

For the gravy:

2 tablespoons butter

1 onion, finely diced

1 1/2 teaspoons. all-purpose flour

1 cup milk

Salt and pepper to taste

Because of rationing during World War II, sausages were made with water so they would often whistle, sputter, and then explode in the pan under high heat.

Bang!

In a large, oiled frying pan at medium heat, fry the sausages, turning them from time to time, until firm and golden brown - about 20 minutes. Set aside and keep warm.

Place potatoes in a large saucepan, with salted water to cover, and bring to a boil over medium heat. Cook for about 15 minutes or until potatoes are tender when pierced with a fork. Drain and pass the potatoes through a ricer. Add milk and butter and beat until smooth. Season with salt and pepper.

In saucepan over low heat, melt the butter. Add flour, onions, salt and pepper and cook until smooth. Stir in milk. Heat to boiling on medium heat, stirring constantly for 1 minute.

Divide the sausages and mash equally among individual plates. Spoon gravy on top and serve immediately.

Serves 4.

Tied-Up, Stuffed, and Rolled
(Briciole)

1/2 cup dried bread crumbs

1 garlic clove, minced

2/3 cup grated Pecorino Romano

1/3 cup provolone, grated

2 tablespoons fresh Italian parsley leaves, chopped

4 tablespoons olive oil

Salt and pepper

1 to 1-1/2-pound flank steak

4 slices prosciutto

1 cup red wine

3 1/4 cups marinara sauce

Most players in Roller Derby leagues skate under pseudonyms, many of which are creative examples of word play with mock-violent or sexual puns.

One local team features player names like Bette Churass, Busty Pipes, June CleaveHer, and Fetishly Divine.

Preheat the oven to 350°F.

In a medium bowl, combine bread crumbs, Pecorino Romano, Provolone, Italian parsley, olive oil and salt and black pepper. Stir well and set aside.

On a cutting board, lay the flank steak out flat. Evenly distribute the bread crumb mixture over the steak. Add a layer of prosciutto. Roll up the steak like a jelly roll being sure to completely enclose the filling. Tie the steak roll using butcher's twine.

Season with salt and pepper.

In a medium-size dutch oven, heat 2 tablespoons of oil over medium heat. Cook the braciole making quarter turns until browned on all sides. Add marinara sauce and wine and bring to a boil. Cover and bake for 1 hour and 20 minutes, the last half hour uncovered.

Cut the briciole into 3/4-inch-thick slices. Serve with the sauce.

Horny
(Grilled Mojo-Marinated Skirt Steak)

2 pounds skirt steak, trimmed

2 tablespoons lime juice

1/4 cup orange juice

1/4 cup onion, diced

2/3 cup olive oil, divided

4 medium cloves garlic, minced

1/2 teaspoon dried oregano

1 teaspoon ground cumin

1 teaspoon dried cilantro

Salt and black pepper

The aptly named Horny Goat Weed is a flowering perennial found mainly in China. The plant contains icariin, which is a PDE5 inhibitor like sildenafil, the active ingredient of Viagra. It holds an important place in traditional Chinese medicine as an aphrodisiac and a treatment for erectile dysfunction.

Preheat gas grill to high heat.

In a resealable bag add skirt steak, lime juice, orange juice, onion, olive oil, garlic, oregano, cumin, cilantro, salt, and pepper. Seal and put in the refrigerator to marinate for a minimum of one hour, but preferably overnight.

Remove meat from bag and pat dry with paper towels.

Simmer marinade in a small saucepan over medium heat until reduced by half.

Place steak on grill flipping occasionally until well-charred and to your wellness preference. Allow to rest for 10 minutes before slicing against the grain.

Serve with pan sauce reduction.

Serves 4

Smells Like Fish

That's because it is fish, silly!

Mussels in White Wine

·

Fish Taco with Tomatillo Guacamole

·

Fish Fry

·

Seafood Chowder

·

Crab and Shrimp Étouffée

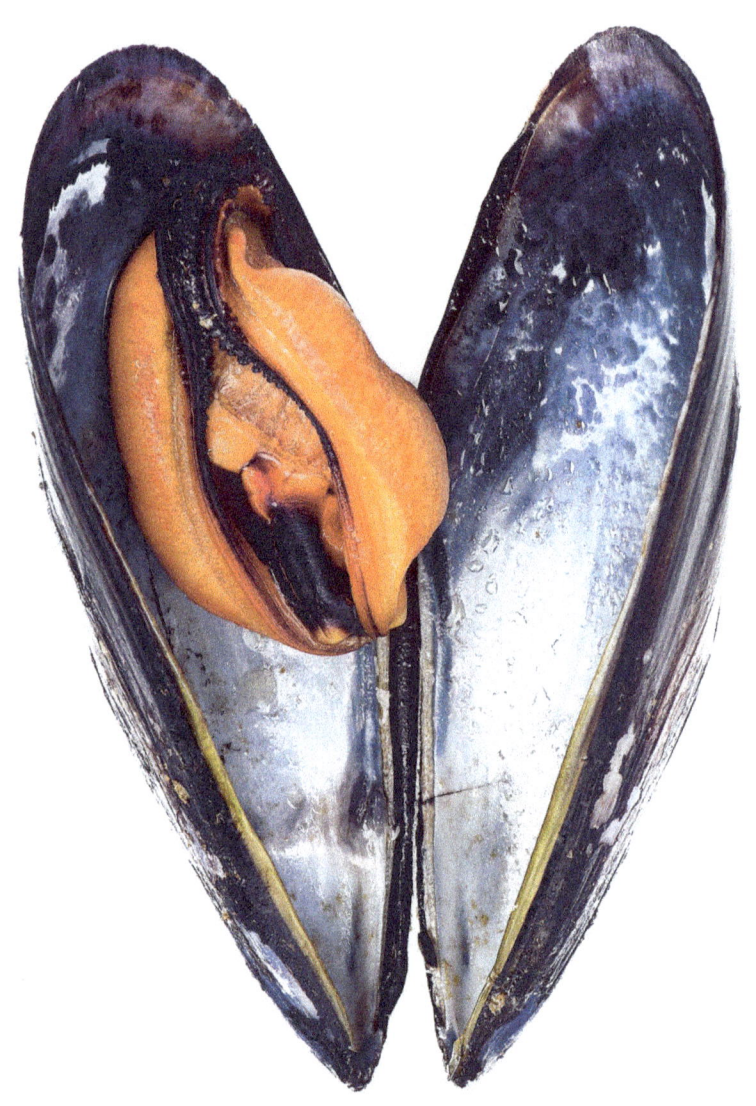

Love Mussel

2 pounds live mussels, beard removed
1 tablespoon butter
2 scallions, chopped
2 cloves garlic, chopped
1/4 teaspoon saffron thread, crushed
3/4 cup dry white wine

Mussels are edible bivalves of the marine family Mytilidae, most of which live on exposed shores in the intertidal zone, attached by means of their strong byssal threads to a firm substrate.

So, what's not to love?

In a Dutch oven over medium-high heat, melt the butter and saute the scallions and garlic.

Add the white wine and bring it to a boil. Add saffron and the mussels in a single layer and cover the pot.

Allow the mussels to steam for 5 minutes. Throw out any mussels that didn't open.

Fish Taco
(with Tomatillo Guacamole)

"When you come to a fork in the road, take it."
 - Lawrence Peter Berra

"When you come to a "Y" in the road, eat it with a fork."
 - Anonymous

Prepare a grill to high heat.

Boil tomatillos in a pot of water for 5 minutes. Allow to cool.

Cut avocado in half and remove the pit. Scoop into a medium bowl and mash with the tomatillo, sour cream, jalapeño, onion, cilantro and lime juice. Season with salt and pepper.

Brush the fish with oil and season with salt and pepper. Grill until lightly charred and cooked through - approximately 10 minutes. Remove the skin.

Spoon a dollop of guacamole on a tortilla. Top with fish, diced tomato and shredded cabbage. Serve with lime wedges and hot sauce.

4 tomatillos, husked and rinsed

2 ripe avocados

1/2 cup sour cream

1 jalapeño, seeded and thinly sliced

1/2 cup onion, minced

1/2 cup cilantro, chopped

5 tablespoons fresh lime juice

Salt and pepper

2 cups Napa cabbage, shredded

Olive oil for brushing

2 pounds Haddock fillets with skin,

8 -7-inch flour tortillas, warmed

Lime wedges

Hot sauce

WTF
(Wednesday, Thursday, Friday Fish Fry)

1/4 teaspoon salt

1/4 teaspoon ground black pepper

1/4 teaspoon garlic powder

1/4 teaspoon cayenne pepper

1/4 teaspoon paprika

2 cups all-purpose flour, divided

1/2 cup cornstarch

1-1/2 teaspoons baking powder

1 (12-ounce) bottle beer

4 cod fillets (6 ounces each)

Wedged lemons for topping

WTF is nothing more than a countdown to Friday's dinner.

In a large bowl, mix together 1 1/2 cups flour, cornstarch, baking powder, garlic powder, cayenne pepper, paprika, salt, and black pepper. Add beer and whisk until smooth.

Prepare a pie tin or shallow bowl with the 1/2 cup of remaining flour.

After patting the cod fish dry, coat it in the beer batter and then dredge in flour. With vegetable oil heated to 375°F in a large cast iron skillet, fry fish, turning frequently. Cook until golden - approximately 4 to 5 minutes.

Place cooked fish on paper towel-lined baking sheet to absorb excess oil. Serve with lemon wedges.

Sea Men
(Manly Seafood Chowder)

Captain Meriwether Lewis had a black Newfoundland dog named Seamen. During their famed expedition from the Atlantic coast to the Pacific coast and back, Lewis & Clark's Corps of Discovery ate over 200 other dogs, but they didn't eat Seamen.

In a large soup kettle, add water, wine, potatoes, onions, celery, bay leaves, garlic, and thyme. Bring to a boil and cook for 10 minutes.

Add the scallops, lobster, shrimp, cod and lump crab. Cook for 10 minutes. Add the butter, salt, pepper, parsley and cream. Cook for an additional 5 minutes.

With a rod and reel, fish out the bay leaves and serve.

1/4 pound sliced bacon, diced
1 medium onion, chopped
3 cups cubed peeled potatoes
1/4 cup chopped celery
1 1/2 cups water
1/2 cup dry white wine
4 bay leaves
1 teaspoon chopped garlic
1/2 teaspoon fresh thyme
1/2 pound bay or sea scallops, quartered
1/2 pound lobster meat, cut into 1-inch pieces
1/2 pound uncooked medium shrimp, peeled and deveined
1/2 pound cod, cut into 1-inch pieces
1/2 pound lump crab, rough chopped
1/4 cup butter, melted
2 teaspoons salt
1 teaspoon black pepper
2 teaspoons minced fresh parsley
1 pint heavy cream
1 pint Half and Half

Good in Bed
(Crab and Shrimp Étouffée)

1/4 cup butter

2 tablespoons olive oil

1/3 cup all-purpose flour

2/3 cup chopped onion

1/4 cup chopped green bell pepper

1/4 cup chopped celery

3 garlic cloves, minced

14 ounces chicken broth

1/3 cup dry white wine

1 tablespoon Creole seasoning

1 tablespoon tomato paste

1 tablespoon chopped fresh parsley

2 teaspoons Worcestershire sauce

1/2 teaspoon hot sauce

2 pounds medium-size raw shrimp

1 pound fresh crabmeat

5 cups hot cooked long-grain rice

Feeling crabby lately? Here is the Mayo Clinic's list of tips for getting a good night's sleep in your bed.

1. Stick to a sleep schedule. Go to bed and get up at the same time every day, even on weekends, holidays and days off.
2. Pay attention to what you eat and drink. Don't go to bed either hungry or stuffed.
3. Create a bedtime ritual. Do the same things each night to tell your body it's time to wind down.
4. Get comfortable. Create a room that's cool, dark and quiet.
5. Limit daytime naps.
6. Include physical activity in your daily routine.
7. Manage stress. Start with the basics, such as getting organized, setting priorities and delegating tasks.

For tips on how to be good in someone else's bed, check the internet.

In a large Dutch oven over medium-high heat, melt butter with oil and stir in flour. Stir continually until caramel colored – approximately 5 minutes. Add onion, green pepper, celery, and garlic, constantly stirring until vegetables are tender – about 5 minutes.

Stir in chicken broth, white wine, Creole seasoning, tomato paste, parsley, Worcestershire sauce, and hot sauce and cook for 10 minutes. Add shrimp and crabmeat. Cover, reduce heat, and simmer for another 5 minutes.

Serve on a bed of rice.

Lingerie Stretchers

Ponchos are sexy

Blueberry Buckle with Whipped Cream

•

Cream-Filled Long Johns

•

Sticky Buns

•

Jello-Filled Melon Slices

•

Custard Cup

•

Gingerbread Man Cookies

•

Baklava

Buckle and Whipped
(Blueberry Buckle with Whipped Cream)

"Fasten your seatbelts. It's going to be a bumpy night."
 - Bette Davis in All About Eve (1950)

In a large bowl, thoroughly mix sugar, shortening, eggs, milk, flour, baking powder, salt, nutmeg and cloves.

Gently fold in blueberries

Pour batter into a 9-inch greased square pan.

In a separate bowl, combine sugar, vanilla extract, flour, cinnamon, and butter and mix until it resembles coarse crumbs. Distribute crumbs evenly over batter.

Bake for 45- 50 minutes or a toothpick inserts cleanly.

Cut into squares and top with whipped cream.

Yield: 1 9-inch cake

3/4 cup sugar
1/4 cup shortening
2 eggs
1/2 cup milk
1-1/2 cups all-purpose flour
2 teaspoons baking powder
1/2 teaspoon salt
1/4 teaspoon ground nutmeg
1-1/2 cups blueberries
1/2 cup sugar
1/4 teaspoon vanilla extract
1/3 cup flour
1/2 teaspoon ground cinnamon
1/4 cup soft butter

Cream-Filled Long Johns

In a Dutch oven, heat oil that's at least 2 1/2 inches deep to 375°F. Line a large plate with paper towels.

In a stand mixer, add 1 1/2 cups flour, sugar, shortening, eggs, and milk. Mix at low speed, stirring in remaining flour.

Turn the dough on to a well-floured surface. Roll around lightly to coat with flour. Roll dough into a rectangle that's about 3/8 inch thick. Slice the dough into 12 even pieces.

With wide spatula, slide doughnuts into hot oil, turning them when they rise to the surface. Cook 2 to 3 minutes or until golden brown on both sides. Drain on paper towels.

In bowl of stand mixer fitted with whisk beater, place butter and powdered sugar. Beat on low speed until well mixed. Increase speed to high; beat about 4 minutes or until soft and fluffy. Scrape down bowl. Add milk and vanilla; beat 4 minutes longer. Set aside.

To fill donuts, first create a hole thru the length of the long john using the handle of a wooden spoon. Using a pastry bag, squeeze enough vanilla cream into each doughnut to fill the hole.

Place the chocolate chips, butter, corn syrup, and water in a medium bowl. Melt in 20 second increments in the microwave, stirring after each time, until completely melted and smooth. Dip tops in glaze while warm.

If you eat all two dozen of theses doughnuts yourself, next winter be prepared to buy the next size Long Johns.

Canola oil for deep frying

3 1/2 cups self-rising flour
1 cup sugar
2 tablespoons soft shortening
2 eggs
3/4 cup milk

Vanilla Cream Filling:
1 cup butter, softened
3 cups powdered sugar
2 tablespoons whole milk
1/2 teaspoon vanilla extract

Chocolate Glaze:
1/2 cup semi-sweet chocolate chips
2 tablespoons butter
2 teaspoons light corn syrup
2 teaspoons water

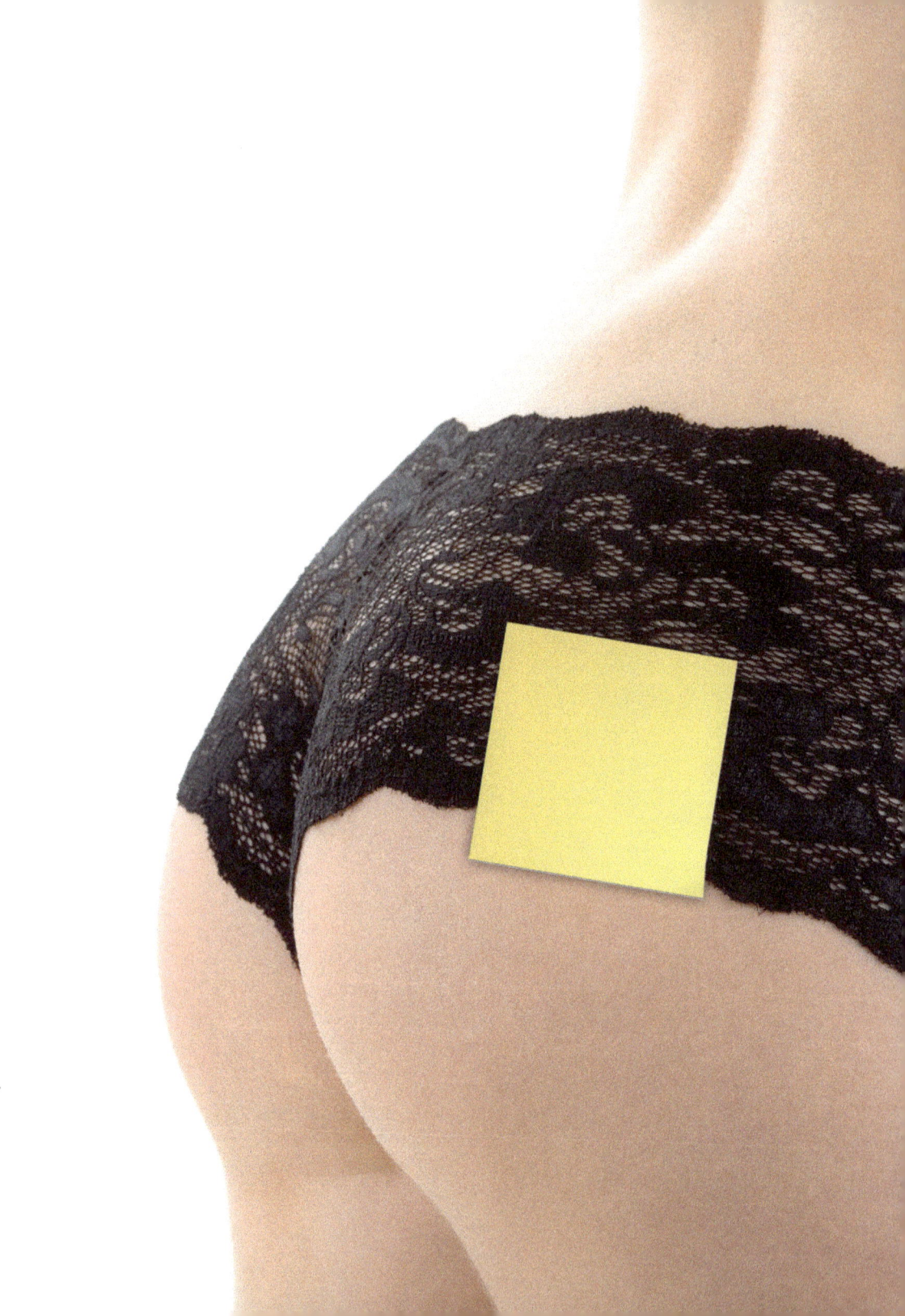

Sticky Buns

1/4 cup butter

1/4 cup packed dark brown sugar

3 tablespoons honey

1/4 cup heavy cream

1/4 cup chopped pecans

Buns

3 tablespoons butter, melted

1/3 cup granulated sugar

1/2 teaspoon ground cinnamon

1 can (7.5 ounce) refrigerated buttermilk biscuits

Caution: These are not called sticky buns because the buns have an adhesive quality. They get their name because if you eat too many, it sticks to your buns.

Preheat oven to 375°F.

In a medium sized bowl, mix melted butter, brown sugar, honey, and heavy cream until well blended. Pour into an 8-inch round pan and cover with pecans.

In small bowl, place 3 tablespoons melted butter. In another small bowl, mix granulated sugar and cinnamon.

Separate dough and dip each piece first into melted butter to coat all sides, and then into sugar mixture, coating well. Arrange dough, sides touching, over topping in pan.

Bake 18 to 22 minutes, or until golden brown. Allow 2 minutes before turning the pan upside down onto heatproof serving plate. Let pan remain for a minute before removing to allow the caramel and nuts to ooze over the rolls.

Serve warm.

Yield: 12 buns

Jiggly Melons
(Jello Filled Melon Slices)

A melon is any of various plants of the family Cucurbitaceae with edible, fleshy fruit.

There are dozens of varieties, including the honeydew, casaba, cantaloupe, watermelon, jugs, boobies, hooters, knockers, and double lattes.

Boil 1 cup of water.

Cut melon in half lengthwise, and then cut a thin slice off bottom of each half to help it to stand upright. Using a large spoon, remove the seeds and any excess moisture. Pat the insides dry with paper towels.

In a medium-size bowl, dissolve the raspberry Jello in the boiling water, stirring until completely dissolved. Mix in 1 cup cold water and refrigerate for an hour to partially set the Jello mixture.

Carefully spoon the partially-set Jello into the center of each melon. Refrigerate 4 hours or overnight to firmly set.

Cut each melon into wedges or slices.

Makes two hand fulls.

1 medium-size melon
1 (3-ounce) package raspberry Jello
1 cup boiling water
1 cup cold water

C-Cup
(Custard Cup)

Eating custard from a c-cup is a happy medium between too small and too large a serving.

Preheat oven to 300°F.

Place six 4-ounce ramekins in a deep baking pan.
In a medium saucepan, bring the milk to a simmer over medium-low heat.

In a medium-size bowl, whisk together the eggs, yolks, sugar, vanilla and salt. Very slowly whisk the egg mixture into the simmering milk. Pour the mixture into the ramekins and sprinkle each one with orange zest.

Fill the pan with hot water to half the height of the ramekins. Bake on the center rack for 30 to 35 minutes or until the custard is firm.

Allow to cool before serving.

Serves 3 pair.

3 eggs plus 3 yokes

1/3 cup granulated sugar

1 teaspoon pure vanilla extract

Pinch salt

3 cups milk, heated until hot, not boiling

1/4 teaspoon orange or lemon zest

Man With Heart On
(Gingerbread Man Cookies)

3/4 cup packed dark brown sugar

1 stick butter, softened

2 large eggs

1/4 cup molasses

3 3/4 cups all-purpose flour, plus more for dusting work surface

2 teaspoons ground ginger

1 1/2 teaspoons baking soda

1/2 teaspoon ground cinnamon

1/2 teaspoon freshly grated nutmeg

1/2 teaspoon salt

Icing:

1 cup confectioners' sugar, sifted

2 tablespoons milk

Right up until the mid-nineteenth century, in some small Villages in England, gingerbread men were thought to have magical properties. Unmarried women were instructed to eat gingerbread "husbands" so they would stand a good chance of meeting a real one.

Preheat the oven to 350°F. Line cookie sheets with parchment paper.

Using a stand mixer at low speed, cream the sugar and butter. Mix in the eggs and molasses. Sift together the flour, ginger, baking soda, cinnamon, nutmeg, and salt. Combine the dry ingredients with the butter mixture.

Wrap the dough in plastic and refrigerate for about 1 hour.

Cut the dough into 4 pieces and allow it to sit at room temperature until pliable - about 15 minutes. Take about 1/4 of the dough and roll it onto a floured work surface until about 1/8-inch thick. Cut out with gingerbread man cookie cutters. Transfer the cookies to the prepared cookie sheets.

Bake until just beginning to brown at the edges – about 10 minutes. Transfer to wire racks to cool.

In a small bowl, mix together the confectioners' sugar and milk. Divide into smaller bowls and use different color food coloring . Decorate by piping eyes, mouths, whips, buckles, and handcuffs.

Honey Between the Sheets
(Baklava)

In the Old Testament, King Solomon said, "My son, eat thou honey, for it is good."

The modern version of this can be found on t-shirts, posters, and bumper stickers: Bee healthy. Eat your honey.

Preheat oven to 350°F. Thoroughly butter a 9 x 13 inch rectangular baking dish.

In a medium bowl, combine walnuts, cinnamon, cardamom and cloves and set aside.

In the baking dish, layer 8-12 sheets of phyllo dough, brushing every other one with butter before adding the next. Press lightly into the pan. Sprinkle on enough of the nut mixture over the dough to make a single layer.

Repeat the dough and nut layering three times, plus 4 more buttered phyllo sheets, ending with a buttered top.

Cut into 1 1/2 inch squares. Bake until the baklava is a golden brown- about 45 minutes.

In a small saucepan, bring to a boil 1 stick of the butter, honey, water, sugar, and vanilla, and then reduce the heat to low.

Pour the syrup over the warm baklava and allow it to absorb overnight. Garnish with nuts.

3 cups walnuts, finely chopped
1 cup pistachios, finely chopped
1 teaspoon ground cinnamon
1/2 teaspoon ground cardamom
1/4 teaspoon ground cloves
1 pound package phyllo sheets, thawed
1/2 cup butter, melted

Syrup:
1 stick butter
2 cups honey
1/2 cup water
1/2 cup sugar
2 teaspoons vanilla extract

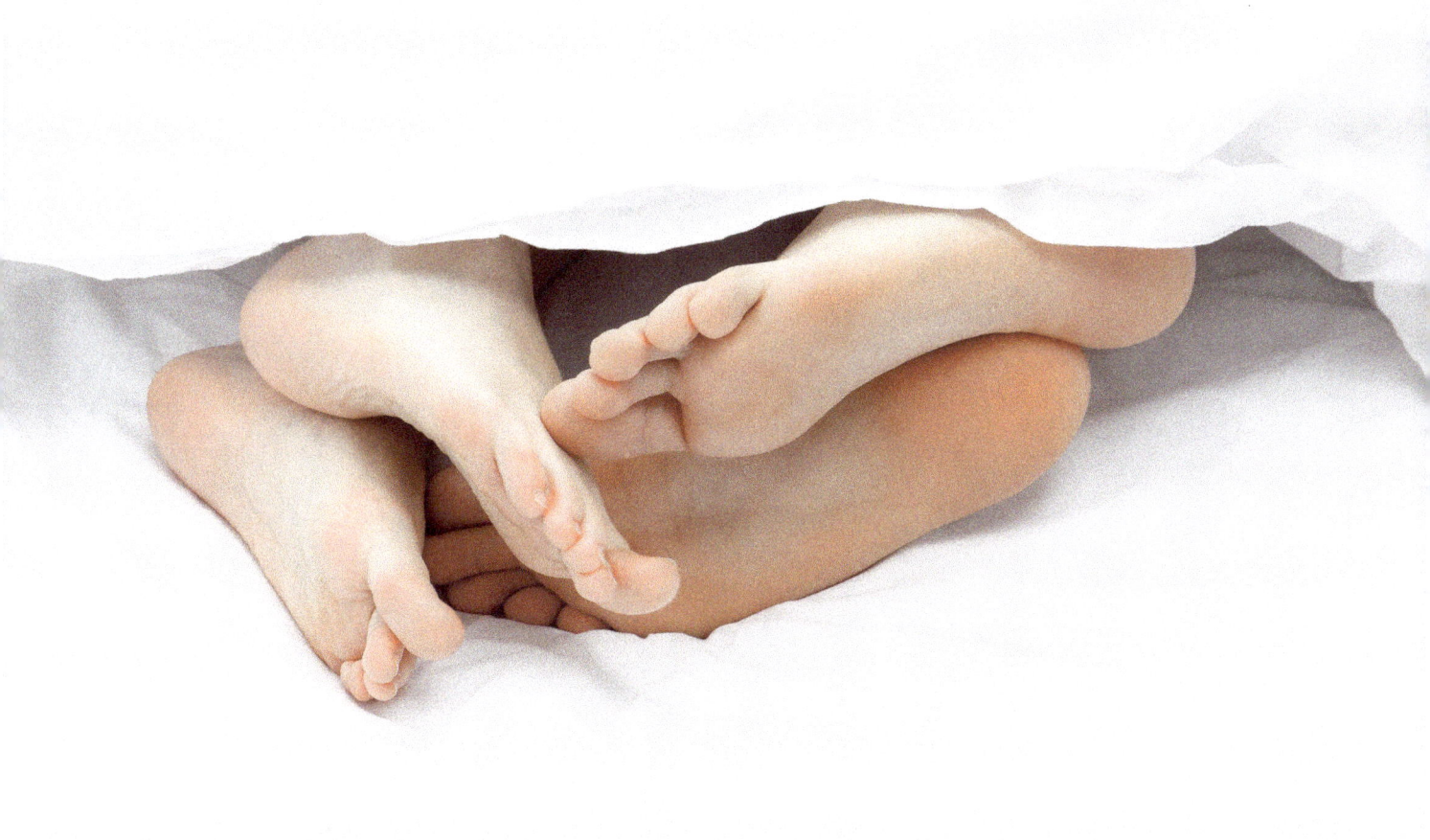

Foreplay

Rubs, marinades, and sauces to pickle, tickle, and bring your limp meat back to life

Jerk Sauce
·
Rib Sauce
·
Butt Rub
·
Horseradish Sauce
·
Mayonnaise

Jerk Sauce

Very popular in the 20's, 30's and well into the 50's, the Soda Jerk was the fountain attendant in a drugstore. Working much like a non-alcohol bartender, he would serve-up phosphates, rickeys, and ice cream sodas.

The name soda jerk came from the "jerking" action the server would use to swing the pipe-like soda fountain handle back and forth when adding the soda water.

Place all ingredients in a blender. Blend until almost smooth.

1 cup ketchup
3 tablespoons soy sauce
3 tablespoons dark rum
1/2 cup cider vinegar
10 green onions, chopped
4 garlic cloves, peeled, chopped
2 tablespoons dried thyme
2 habanero chiles with seeds, chopped
2 tablespoons vegetable oil
2 teaspoons dark brown sugar
4 teaspoons ground allspice
4 teaspoons ground ginger
4 teaspoons ground cinnamon
2 teaspoons ground nutmeg
2 teaspoons salt
2 teaspoons ground black pepper

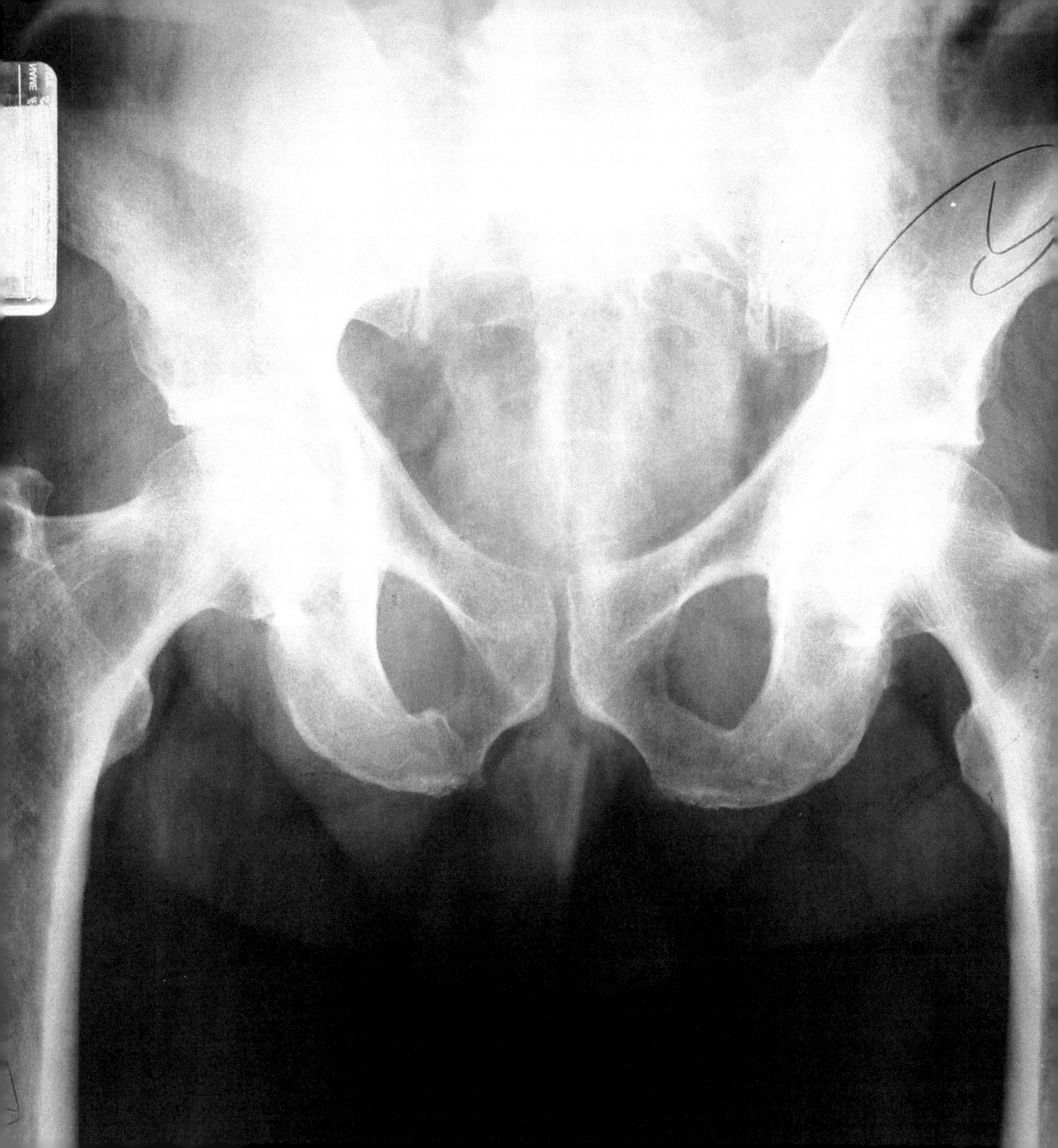

Baby Got Back
(Rib Sauce)

1 1/4 cup ketchup

1 cup water

1/3 cup cider vinegar

1/4 cup dark brown sugar

2 tablespoons molasses

1 tablespoon onion powder

1 tablespoon garlic powder

1 tablespoon black pepper

1 teaspoon celery salt

1 teaspoon allspice

1 teaspoon cayenne

The central feature of the human back is the vertebral column, specifically the length from the top of the thoracic vertebrae to the bottom of the lumbar vertebrae, which houses the spinal cord in its spinal canal. The width of the back at the top is defined by the scapula, the broad, flat bones of the shoulders.

So anatomically speaking, Sir Mix-a-Lot's 1993 Grammy Award winning song "Baby Got Back" which is about the rapper's attraction to very large buttocks, is well south of the mark.

In a medium saucepan combine all ingredients over a medium heat, constantly stirring for 5 minutes.

Lower heat and simmer for 20 minutes and sauce is thick.

Butt Rub
(Memphis-Style Pork Butt, Ribs, or Shoulder Rub)

This recipe is good for when you're getting a little behind in your work.

Mix ingredients together in bowl.

Coat with cooking oil meat before applying rub.

Liberally apply rub 2 to 4 hours before cooking.

A little lower and to the left. Ahhhh.

1/4 cup dark brown sugar

1/4 cup paprika

1 tablespoon mustard powder

1 tablespoon onion powder

1 tablespoon garlic powder

1 tablespoon dried basil

1/2 teaspoon ground bay leaves

1-1/2 teaspoons dried thyme

1 teaspoon ground cumin

2 tablespoons Lawry's seasoned salt

1/2 teaspoon dried orange peel

2 teaspoons coarse black pepper

1 teaspoon cayenne pepper

1/2 teaspoon rosemary powder

2 tablespoons chili powder

...and the Horse You Rode In On
(Horseradish Sauce)

1 1/2 cups sour cream

1/2 cup prepared white horseradish

6 tablespoons chopped fresh chives

4 teaspoons fresh lemon juice

Salt and black pepper

Some jokes or anecdotes are deservedly forgotten, but the punch lines, or portions of them, live on.

In the background of the oil painting that hangs as the official portrait of Donald Regan, who served as Secretary of the Treasury in the Reagan Administration, can be found a book titled "And the Horse You Rode In On." No other book title is visible.

"On Language; Of High Moments and The Horse You Rode In On"
- William Safire, NY Times - June 28, 1998

Whisk all ingredients to blend in small bowl. Season with salt and pepper.

Made By Guys With Their Stick
(Mayonnaise)

1 extra large egg

2 teaspoons lemon juice

1/4 teaspoon salt

1/2 teaspoon Dijon mustard

1 cup extra light tasting olive oil

1 teaspoon white-wine vinegar

Equipment Required:

A stick immersion blender

One pint Mason jar

If you've got a stick, you can make it by the jar-full.

Add all the ingredients to a 1 pint Mason jar .

Insert a stick immersion blender all the way down to the bottom of the jar.

Blend at the bottom of the jar for a full 20 seconds. The oil will begin to thicken, gradually transforming all the way to the top of the jar.

Lasts for up to 2 weeks in the refrigerator in an airtight container.

Love Potions

Seductive Sips That Make Any Date Look Better

Lost Virginity
·
Strawberry Milk
·
Lucky Charms Martinis
·
Feeling Merry

Lost Virginity

Pour celery salt on a small plate. With a lemon wedge moisten the rim of a tall glass. Press the rim of the glass in the celery salt until fully coated. Fill the glass with ice. Add one cherry and set aside.

In a cocktail mixer full of ice, combine the tomato juice, Tabasco sauce, horseradish, Worcestershire sauce, celery salt, and black pepper.

If you stopped right here, you'd have a wonderful Virgin Bloody Mary.

Add vodka.

Shake vigorously and strain into the glass.

Remove cherry.

Celery salt to cover small plate

1 Lemon wedge

Ice

4 ounces tomato juice

2 dashes Tabasco Sauce

1 teaspoon horseradish

1 dash Worcestershire sauce

1 pinch Celery salt

1 pinch Ground black pepper

2 ounces Vodka

Fruity Homo Milk
(Strawberry Homogenized Milk)

1 cup strawberries, chopped

1/2 cup sugar

1 cup water

1 1/2 cup whole milk

In a small pot, boil strawberries, sugar and water for about 10 minutes; mixture will reduce and thicken slightly. Using a fine sieve, strain the mixture into a small bowl and set aside until cool

Stir 3 tablespoons of the strawberry syrup into each glass of milk.

Serves 2 people in a loving relationship.

Getting Lucky
(Lucky Charms Martinis)

These martinis are magically delicious.

Separate the marshmallows from the Lucky Charms cereal.

Place 6 Lucky Charms marshmallows of the same color in each of 6 shot glasses. Pink marshmallows in one shot glass, yellow in another, and so on.

Pour one ounce of vodka into each shot glass. Let the marshmallows dissolve.

Serve as vodka shots or mix into your favorite sweet martini recipe!

Your friends will always be after them.

2 cups Lucky Charms cereal
6 ounces flavored vodka
 (whipped cream or
 marshmallow flavor)

Feeling Merry
(Holiday Drink)

It was a great holiday party, and everyone felt Mary.

Everyone.

Mix all liquids in a tall ceramic mug.
Top with whipped cream.

Find Mary.

1 1/2 ounces Cognac

1 1/2 ounces Kahlua

1 1/2 ounces Baileys Mint Chocolate Cream Liqueur

6 ounces hot chocolate

3 drops vanilla extract

Whipped cream

Quickies

Wham, Bam, Thank You Ma'am

Hot Pockets
·
Spaghetti and Meatballs
·
Parmesan Dill Rolls
·
Spiced Mixed Nuts
·
Chipotle and Lime Chip Dip

Hot Pockets

Despite the name, these sandwiches do not store well in your jeans.

Preheat oven to 350°F.

In a stand mixer, combine flour, dry milk, sugar, salt, yeast, and water and knead well.

Divide dough into 10 equal portions and roll each into a rectangle. Top with cheese and meat and create a pocket by folding sides and ends up.

Place on a prepared cookie sheet, top liberally with Parmesan cheese and garlic powder, and bake for 15-20 minutes or until lightly brown.

Serve warm.

3 cups all-purpose flour

1/4 cup dry milk

1/4 cup sugar

1 teaspoon salt

2 1/2 tablespoons yeast

1 cup warm water

2 cups diced meat

2 cups cheese, shredded

Parmesan cheese

Garlic powder

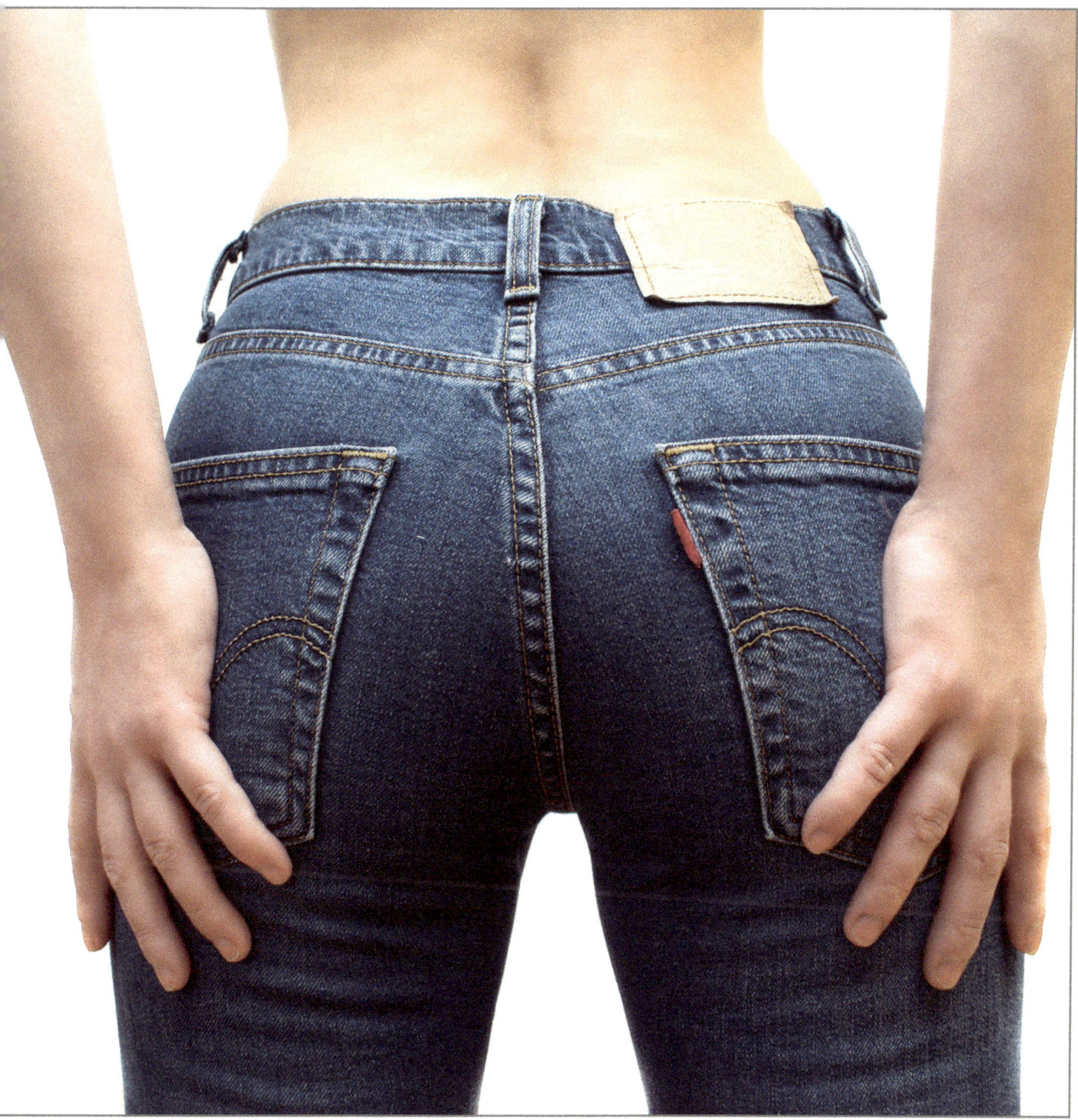

S & M
(Spaghetti and Meatballs)

For Sauce:
1/2 cup minced onion
2 cloves garlic, crushed
2 tablespoons extra-virgin olive oil
1 (28 ounce) can crushed tomatoes
2 (6 ounce) cans tomato paste
2 (6.5 ounce) cans tomato sauce
1/2 cup water
1 1/2 teaspoons dried basil
1/2 teaspoon fennel seed
1 teaspoon Italian seasoning
1/2 teaspoon salt
1/4 teaspoon ground black pepper

For Meatballs:
8 ounces 85% ground beef
8 ounces ground pork
1/2 cup fresh breadcrumbs
1 cup whole milk ricotta cheese
1/2 cup Parmigiano-Reggiano, grated
1/4 cup Italian parsley, chopped
1 teaspoon salt
1/4 teaspoon ground black pepper
2 large garlic cloves, minced
1/2 onion, minced
2 large eggs

1 pound spaghetti

In many families, Wednesday night is their traditional S&M night.

In a large pot, combine onion, garlic, crushed tomatoes, tomato paste, tomato sauce, water, dried basil, fennel seed, Italian seasoning, salt and pepper. Simmer at a low heat setting for 2 hours, stirring occasionally.

In a large bowl, mix beef, pork, breadcrumbs, ricotta cheese, Parmigiano-Reggiano, parsley, salt, pepper, onion, and garlic. In a small bowl, whisk eggs and add to meat mixture.

Roll mixture between palms into golf-ball-size meatballs, and arrange in a single layer in sauce in pot. Simmer 15 to 20 minutes until meatballs are cooked through.

In large pot of boiling salted water, cook spaghetti until just tender but still firm to bite, stirring occasionally. Drain.

Transfer meatballs to platter using a slotted spoon and add pasta to sauce in pot and toss to coat.

Divide spaghetti equally among 6 plates and top each serving with meatballs.

Sprinkle with freshly grated Parmigiano-Reggiano cheese and serve.

Dill Dough
(Parmesan Dill Rolls)

1/4 cup butter

1/3 cup milk

3 tablespoons water

1 pinch salt

2/3 cup self-rising flour

2 eggs

1 1/2 teaspoons dried dill weed

1 cup grated Parmesan cheese

This faux obituary has recently blanketed the interweb:

Sad news.

Please join me in remembering yet another great icon of the entertainment community. The Pillsbury Dough Boy died yesterday of a yeast infection and traumatic complications from repeated pokes to the belly. He was 71.

Dough Boy is survived by his wife, Play Dough and three children, John Dough, Jane Dough, and Dill Dough, plus they had one in the oven. Service was held at 3:50 for about 20 minutes.

Preheat oven to 450°F. Lightly grease a baking sheet.

In a small saucepan, heat butter, milk, water and salt over medium-high heat. When butter has melted, pour mixture into a large bowl.

Add flour and stir well. Mix in eggs, dill and Parmesan cheese. Stir until a loose batter is formed.

Work the dough until satisfied. Drop large spoonfuls of batter onto prepared baking sheet.

Bake in preheated oven until golden, about 18 to 20 minutes.

Yields 10 rolls. Serve yourself.

Playing With Your Nuts
(Spiced Mixed Nuts)

Defend Your Nuts is a defensive shooting game available as a smartphone app. It stars a cute squirrel who must defend his acorns against waves of evil monsters!

Warning: Onlookers become very annoyed if you begin playing this game before you remove your phone from your pocket.

Preheat oven to 350°F. Line a baking sheet with aluminum foil and lightly coat with cooking spray.

In a large bowl combine walnut halves, pecan halves, almonds, cashews, salt, black pepper, cumin, and cayenne pepper and toss to coat.

In a small saucepan mix sugar, water, and butter. Cook over medium heat until the butter is melted. Slowly pour butter mixture over the bowl of nuts and stir to coat.

Spread nuts in a single layer on a prepared baking sheet.

Bake for 10 minutes until nuts are tacky and roasted. Cool before serving.

Cooking spray

1 cup untoasted walnut halves

1 cup untoasted pecan halves

1 cup unsalted, dry roasted almonds

1 cup unsalted, dry roasted cashews

1 teaspoon salt

1/2 teaspoon black pepper

1/4 teaspoon ground cumin

1/4 teaspoon cayenne pepper

1/2 cup white sugar

1/4 cup water

1 tablespoon butter

Easy Lays
(Chipotle and Lime Chip Dip)

2 cups sour cream

1 cup mayonnaise

2 tablespoons chipotle powder

4 teaspoons garlic powder

1 teaspoon salt

1/3 cup lime juice

Lays Potato Chips

This popular treat gets passed around at parties.

In a non-reactive bowl, mix together sour cream, mayonnaise, chipotle powder, garlic powder, salt, and lime juice.

Cover and refrigerate 2 hours to overnight.

Size Matters

5 1/2 inches=   8 inches
1 tablespoon =   8 inches
1/16 cup =   8 inches
1/8 cup =   8 inches
1/4 cup =   8 inches
1/3 cup =   8 inches
3/8 cup =   8 inches
1/2 cup =   8 inches
2/3 cup =   8 inches
3/4 cup =   8 inches
1 cup =   8 inches
1 cup =   8 inches
1 pint =   8 inches
1 quart=   8 inches
4 cups =   8 inches
1 gallon =   8 inches
16 ounces =   8 inches

Index

A
Acorns, 124
Alcohol, 96
Allspice, 35, 96, 99
Almonds, 124
Aluminum foil, 17, 124
Andouille, 20
Antony, Marc, 4
Aphrodisiac, 4, 39, 65
Apple, 25
Applewood, 9, 13
Artichoke, 37, 39
Asiago, 39
Atlanta, 25
Avocado, 9, 19, 70

B
Back, 26, 74, 95-96, 99
Baby Got Back, 99
Bacon, 9, 13, 15, 17, 20, 74
Baileys, 114
Bake, 10, 17, 20, 26, 39-40, 47, 51, 55, 63, 80, 85, 88, 91-92, 118, 123-124
Baklava, 79, 92
Ball, 52, 121
Bamboo, 28
Bangers, 61
Barbecue, 55
Bartender, 96
Basil, 31, 100, 121
Bay, 35, 74, 100
Beaneaters, Boston, 47
Bee, 92
Beef, 25, 28, 35, 52, 55, 121
Beer, 73
Benedict, 9, 19
Berra, Lawrence Peter, 70
Bird, 47, 49
Biscuits, 85
Bivalves, 69
Blanket, 9, 20
Bleu, 47
Bloody, 108
Blueberry, 79-80
Boneless, 28, 39, 44, 47
Boobies, 86
Boston Beaneaters, 47
Boxer, 20
Bra, 44
Bread, 13, 32, 40, 43, 47, 52, 63
Breadcrumbs, 43, 121
Breakfast, 9, 13
Breast, 39, 44, 47
Briciole, 51, 63
Brioche, 19
Broiled, 25
Broth, 40, 51-52, 55, 77
Brouwer, Luitzen Egbertus Jan, 52
Bruce, Lenny, 5
Buckle, 79-80, 91
Buffalo, 1, 25, 131
Bull, 4
Bullpucky, 15
Bun, 25, 79, 85
Burlesque, 43
Busty Pipes, 63
Butcher, 63
Butt, 95, 100
Butter, 40, 43-44, 61, 69, 74, 77, 80, 82, 85, 91-92, 123-124
Buttermilk, 85
Buttocks, 99

C
Cabbage, 25, 70
Caesium, 55
Cake, 80
Canola, 82
Cantaloupe, 86
Capicola, 32
Caramel, 77, 85
Caraway, 25
Carburetor, 17
Cardamom, 92
Carrots, 25
Casaba, 86
Cashews, 124
Casing, 25, 44
Casserole, 40
Cavity, 43, 49
Cayenne, 59, 73, 99-100, 124
Celery, 35, 74, 77, 99, 108
Cereal, 112
Charcoal, 25
Chardonnay, 49
Charms, Lucky, 107, 112,
Cheddar, 35, 55
Cheese, 9-10, 25-26, 35, 39, 43, 47, 55, 118, 121, 123
Cherry, 31, 108
Chicago, 25
Chicken, 5, 37, 39-40, 43-44, 47, 49, 52, 77
Chiles, 96
Chili, 25, 35, 100
China, 65
Chinese, 65
Chip, 82, 117, 127
Chipotle, 117, 127
Chives, 103
Chocolate, 4, 15, 82, 114
Chorizo, 37, 44
Chowder, 67, 74
Christmas, 20
Chuck, 52
Churass, Bette, 63
Ciabatta, 32
Cider, 59, 96, 99
Cilantro, 65, 70
Cinnamon, 35, 80, 85, 91-92, 96
Cinncinatti, 35
Cities, 25
Clark, 74
Classical, 26
CleaveHer, June, 63
Cleopatra, 4
Clove, 28, 35, 43, 49, 55, 63, 65, 69, 77, 80, 92, 96, 121
Club, 40, 56
Cock, 7
Cocktail, 108
Cocoa, 35
Coconut, 52
Cod, 73-74
Cognac, 114
Coleslaw, 25
Comedy, 13
Commando, 20
Condiments, 25
Condominiums, 13
Confectioners, 91
Consummation, 4
Cookie, 20, 79, 91, 118
Corn, 37, 39, 82
Corned, 25
Cornstarch, 73
Corps, 74
Courtship, 4
Coventry, 40
Cowlick, 52
Crab, 67, 74, 77
Crack, 19
Cranium, 28
Cream, 55, 70, 74, 79-80, 82, 85, 91, 96, 103, 112, 114, 127
Creepy, 7, 131
Creole, 77
Crescent, 20
Crumbs, 39-40, 43, 47, 52, 63, 80
Crust, 37, 39
Cumin, 28, 35, 65, 100, 124
Custard, 79, 88

D
Dancing, 56
Davis, Bette, 80
Dawn, 19
Decorate, 91
Defend Your Nuts, 124
Deux, 35
Deveined, 74
Diamond, 15
Dijon, 39, 105
Dill Dough, 117, 123
Dip, 13, 28, 39, 82, 85, 117, 127
Divine, Fetishly, 63
Dog, 23, 25, 74
Doggy, 25
Donald, 103
Donnelly, 1-2, 131
Dorothy, 25
Double lattes, 86
Dough, 20, 82, 85, 91-92, 118, 123
Doughnut, 82
Drugstore, 96
Dutch, 63, 69, 77, 82

E
Earl of Mercia, 40
Egg, 9-10, 13, 19-20, 39-40, 43, 47, 80, 82, 88, 105
Emperor, 4
Engine, 17
England, 91
Erect, 49
Erectile disfunction, 65
Esoteric, 5
Étouffée, 77
Evil, 124
Expedition, 74
Explode, 61
Exposed, 69
Extract, 80, 82, 88, 92, 114

F
Fennel, 121
Feta fries, 23, 26
Fetishly Divine, 63
Fillets, 70, 73
Filling, 63, 82
Finger, 47
Fish, 7, 67, 70, 73
Flake, 37, 39
Flank, 63
Floured, 82, 91
Foil, 17, 55, 124
Follically, 52
Foreplay, 7, 95
Fork, 55-56, 61, 70
Fountain, 96
Frank, 25
French toast, 9, 13, 35
Friday, 73
Fried, 13, 25
Fries, 23, 26
Frittatas, 9-10
Fruit, 86
Fruity, 111
Fry, 13, 43, 61, 67, 73

G
Garlic, 26, 28, 35, 39, 43, 49, 52, 55, 59, 63, 65, 69, 73-74, 77, 96, 99-100, 118, 121, 127
Garnish, 52, 92
Gas, 17, 65
Geek, 52
Giants, 47
Gibbons, 13
Giblets, 49
Ginger, 91, 96
Gingerbread, 91
Girl, 31, 43
Glaze, 82
Goat, 65
Godgifu, Tom 40
Godiva, Lady, 40
Going Commando, 20
Golf, 121
Graded, 10
Grain, 65, 77
Grammy Award, 99

Index

G (cont.)
Granulated, 85, 88
Grapes, 4
Greek, 26, 39
Green, 43, 55, 77, 96
Griddle, 25
Grill, 17, 28, 49, 51, 56, 65, 70
Guacamole, 67, 70

H
Habanero, 96
Haddock, 70
Hairy, 52
Half & Half, 13, 20, 32, 43, 49, 55, 63, 65, 70, 74, 86, 88
Halftime, 32
Handcuffs, 91
Hardwood, 25
Harvey, 39
Havarti, 10
Heart, 4, 29, 25, 31, 39, 91
Heaven, 17
Heavy, 19, 40, 74, 85
Hershey, 17
Hide, 32
Hockey, 25
Hog, 17, 59
Holiday, 114
Hollandaise, 9, 19
Homo milk, 111
Honey, 39, 85, 92
Honeydew, 86
Hooters, 86
Horny Goat Weed, 65
Horse, 103
Horseradish, 95, 103, 108
Hot Pockets, 118

I
Icariin, 65
Icing, 91
Immersion blender, 105
Implants, 44
Irish, 31
Iron, 15, 73
Italian, 31-32, 63, 121

J
Jalapeno, 70
Jane Dough, 123
Jar, 49, 105
Jello, 79, 86
Jelly, 63
Jerk, 95-96
Jerking, 96
Jersey, 25
Jiggly, 86
John, 39, 123
Johns, 79, 82
Joke, 43, 103
Jugs, 86
Juice, 19, 26, 39, 49, 65, 70, 103, 105, 108, 127
June, 63, 103
June CleaveHer, 63

K
kabob, 23, 28
Kahlua, 114
Kama Sutra, 9, 15, 17
Kansas, 25
Kellogg, John Harvey, 39
Ketchup, 25, 59, 96, 99
Kilted sausage, 20
Kilts, 20
King Solomon, 92
Kiss, 17
Kleenex, 44
Knead, 118
Knockers, 86
Kosher, 28, 47, 100

L
Laddle, 52
Lzady, 40
Laid, 10, 17
Lattes, 86
Lawrence Peter Berra, 70
Lays, 127
Leaf, 35, 52
Leagues, 63
Lean, 55
Leaves, 39, 63, 74, 100
Leftover, 40
Leg, 37, 43, 49
Legend, 40
Lemon, 19, 26, 39, 49, 73, 88, 103, 105, 108
Lenny, Bruce, 5
Leofric, Earl of Mercia, 40
Lewis, Meriwether, 74
Lime, 65, 70, 117, 127
Limp, 95
Lingerie, 3, 7, 79
Lips, 59
Liqueur, 114
Lizards, 44
Lobster, 74
Love, 4, 7, 15, 25, 69, 107
Lucky, 55, 107, 112
Lucky Charms, 112
Luitzen, 52
Lumbar, 99
Lump, 74

M
Maddog, Dr. 1, 131
Manifold, 17
Mantis, Praying, 4
Maple, 13
Marc, Antony, 4
Marinade, 65, 95
Marinara, 63
Marinate, 28, 51, 65
Marine, 69
Mark, 1-2, 99, 131
Marshmallow, 112
Martinis, 107, 112
Mary, 108, 114
Mashed, 51, 61, 70
Mason jar, 49, 105
Masturbation, 39
Mathematician, 52
Mating, 4
Mayer, Oscar 15
Mayo clinic, 77
Mayonnaise, 95, 105, 127
Meat, 6, 28, 39, 55, 59, 65, 74, 95, 100, 118, 121
Meatballs, 51-52, 117, 121
Medicine, 65
Melon, 86
Menage à Trois, 35
Ménage de Deux, 35
Meriwether Lewis, 74
Merry, 107, 114
Mexican, 44
Microwave, 15, 39, 82
Milk, 10, 40, 61, 80, 82, 88, 91, 107, 111, 118, 121, 123
Mint, 114
Mojo, 51, 65
Molasses, 59, 91, 99
Monks, 4
Monsters, 124
Montezuma, 4
Morningwood Condominiums, 13
Mozzerella, 31
Muffin, 10
Mussel, 69
Mustard, 25, 39, 59, 100, 105
Mytilidae, 69

N
Naked, 40
Napa, 70
Newfoundland, 74
Noodles, 40, 52
Nooners, 6, 23
Nuns, 4
Nurishment, 9
Nutmeg, 35, 80, 91, 96
Nutrition, 3
Nuts, 85, 92, 117, 124

O
Obituary, 123
Obscene, 5
Oil, 19, 26, 28, 31, 35, 43-44, 49, 61, 63, 65, 70, 73, 77, 82, 96, 100, 103, 105, 121
Olive, 19, 26, 28, 31, 35, 44, 49, 63, 65, 70, 77, 105, 121
Onion, 25, 31, 39, 49, 55-56, 61, 65, 70, 77, 99-100, 121
Onlookers, 124
Ooze, 85
Orange, 65, 88, 100
Oregano, 26, 35, 52, 65
Organ, 77
Oscar Mayer's, 15
Oysters, 4

P
Pacific, 74
Painting, 103
Palm, 23, 31
Panchetta, 10, 37, 43
Panko, 40, 47
Pants, 3, 124
Panty, 20
Paprika, 25, 28, 59, 73, 100
Parchment, 91
Paring, 44
Parmesan, 37, 39-40, 43, 47, 117-118, 123
Parmigiano, 47, 52, 121
Parsley, 26, 31, 39, 43, 52, 63, 74, 77, 121
Partner, 59
Party, 114
Pasta, 51-52, 121
Paste, 25, 55, 77, 121
Pastry, 82
PDE5 inhibitor, 65
Pecan, 85, 124

Pecorino, 63
Peel, 26, 61, 74, 96, 100
Peeping, 40
Peppers, 25, 32
Perennial, 65
Peter Gibbons, 13
Philosopher, 52
Phone, 124
Phyllo, 92
Pickle, 25, 95
Pie, 73
Pigs, 9, 20, 59
Pigs in a Blanket, 20
Pillsbury, 20, 123
Pillsbury Dough Boy, 123
Pink, 112
Pipe, 63, 96
Pipes, Busty, 63
Pistachios, 92
Pit, 70
Pitcher, 47
Plant, 65, 86
Plate, 15, 17, 39, 82, 85, 108
Plates, 61, 121
Plumber, 19
Poach, 19
Pocket, 44, 52, 117-118, 124
Poetically, 15
Pokes, 123
Pollution, 39
Ponchos, 79
Porcine, 59
Porcupine, 52
Pork, 51, 52, 59, 61, 121
Posture, 49
Pot, 35, 40, 52, 59, 69-70, 111, 121
Potatoes, 26, 51, 55, 61, 74
Potbellypigs, 59
Potions, 7, 107
Praxiteles, 26
Praying Mantis, 4
Prick, 55
Principal, 43
Processor, 19
Prosciutto, 19, 32, 63
Provolone, 32, 63
Pseudonyms, 63
Pulled pork, 51
Punch, 103
Puns, 63
Puree, 19

Q

Quart, 19, 28, 40, 128
Quarter, 63
Quartered, 74
Quickies, 7

R

Races, 32
Radbourn, Hoss, 47
Radiation, 55
Ramekins, 88
Rapper, 99
Raspberry, 86
Raw, 77
Reagan, Ronald, 103
Reduction, 65
Refrigerate, 31, 85, 86, 91, 127
Refrigerator, 28, 65, 105
Regan, Donald, 103
Reggiano, 47, 52, 121
Regimental, 20
Relish, 25
Reptile, 44
Residence, 13
Reuben, 25
Rib, 95, 99
Rice, 77
Ricer, 61
Rickeys, 96
Ricotta, 37, 43, 121
Rippers, 25
Rival, 47
Road trip, 17
Roast, 32, 43, 59, 124
Roll, 19-20, 39, 55-56, 63, 82, 91, 117-118, 121
Roller Derby, 63
Romano, 63
Romans, 39
Rosemary, 37, 47
Rosie O'Palm, 31
Rub, 95, 100
Rum, 96
Russet, 26, 61

S

Saffron, 69
Safire, William, 103
Sage, 43
Salad, 23, 31
Salami, 23, 32
Sandwich, 9, 13, 23, 32, 51, 56, 118
Sauce, 19, 25, 35, 40, 47, 55-56, 59, 61, 63, 65, 70, 77, 95-96, 99, 103, 108, 121
Sauerkraut, 25
Sausage, 20, 37, 44, 51, 61
Saute, 35, 44, 55, 69
Savory, 25
sayitwithbacon.com, 15
Scallions, 69
Scallops, 74
Scapula, 99
Scientist, 55
Scopas, 26
Scotland, 20
Scottish, 20
Sculpture, 26
Sea, 61, 74
Seafood, 67, 74
Seal, 20, 65
Seamen, 74
Sear, 44
Season, 10, 44, 49, 55, 61, 63, 70, 103, 131
Seconds, 55, 105
Secretary, 103
Seductive, 5, 107
Seed, 35, 121
Seeded, 70, 86, 96
Sex, 4, 23
Sexual, 4-5, 39, 63
Sexy, 3, 5, 79
Shallot, 10, 43
Sheets, 15, 91-92
Shirt, 44
Shooting, 124
Shores, 69
Shortening, 80, 82
Shot, 112
Shredded, 10, 55, 59, 70, 118
Shrimp, 67, 74, 77
Sildenafil, 65
Sir Mix-a-Lot, 99
Sirloin, 28
Skate, 63
Skewers, 28
Skirt, 51, 65
Slang, 5, 20
Sleep, 4, 77
Sloppy, 51, 55
Smoke, 44
Smuggle, 44
Snakes, 44
Soda, 91, 96
Solar, 55
Solomon, King, 92
Song, 99
Soppressata, 32
Soup, 74
Sour, 55, 70, 103, 127
Soy, 96
Spackle, 19
Spaghetti, 35, 52, 117, 121
Spank, 39
Spatula, 82
Spears, 25
Spheres, 52
Spiced, 117, 124
Spinach, 9-10, 37, 39
Spinal, 99
Spread, 43, 124
Sputter, 61
Squirm, 59
Squirrel, 124
Stacked, 25
Statuesque, 131
Steak, 25, 51, 56, 63, 65
Steam, 49, 69
Steamed, 25
Steamies, 25
Stewed, 25
Stick, 15, 28, 40, 77, 91-92, 105
Stock, 52
Stockholm, 44
Stomach, 4
Strawberry, 107, 111
Stress, 77
Stretchers, 7, 79
Strip, 15, 17, 40, 56
Stuff, 7, 43, 44, 49, 67, 131
Stuffed, 37, 39, 43-44, 55, 63
Style, doggy, 25-26
Submarine, 32
Sugar, 31, 80, 82, 85, 88, 91-92, 96, 99-100, 111, 118, 124
Sutra, 9, 15, 17
Sweden, 44
Swing, 96
Swipe, 19
Swiss, 25
Syrup, 13, 82, 92, 111

T

Tabasco, 108
Taco, 67, 70
Tailor, 40
Tangent, 52
Ted's Hot Dogs, 25
Temperature, 31, 49, 56
Tender, 37, 47, 59, 61, 77, 121
Testament, 92
Testicles, 4
Tetrazzini, 37, 40
Theorem, 52
Theories, 39
Thigh, 43, 49
Throne, 37, 49
Thyme, 10, 74, 96, 100
Tickle, 95
Tied, 63
Tighty-whiteys, 20
Toast, 9, 13, 19
Togas, 26
Tom, 40
Tomatillo, 67, 70
Tomato, 25, 31, 35, 55-56, 70, 77, 108, 121
Topology, 52
Topping, 55
Topping, 25, 73, 85
Tortilla, 70
Treasury, 103
Treatment, 65
Trivia, 5
Trois, 35
Turkey, 9, 37, 40
Turmeric, 28
Twice, 51, 55

U

Ultimate, 15
Uncircumcised, 25
Undergarments, 20
Underwear, 20
Undress, 56
Uniform, 20
Unmarried, 91
Unsalted, 124
Unsweetened, 35
Upright, 86

V

Valentine, 4
Vanilla, 80, 82, 88, 92, 114
Vanishing, 52
Veal, 52
Vector, 52
Vegetable, 43, 61, 73, 77, 96
Vertebrae, 99
Viagra, 65
Viet Nam, 20
Villages, 91
Vinaigrette, 31
Vinegar, 19, 28, 31, 59, 96, 99, 105
Virgin, 19, 31, 108, 121
Virginia Woolf, 4
Virginity, 107-108
Vodka, 108, 112
Vulgar, 5

W

Walnut, 92, 124
War, 61
Warning, 124
Waterfront, 131
Watermelon, 86
Website, 15, 59
Wednesday, 73
Weed, 65, 123
Western, 131
Whipped, 79-80, 112, 114
Whips, 91
Whisk, 10, 31, 47, 73, 82, 88, 103, 121
Whiteys, 20
Whore, 55
Wife, 40, 123
Wiggle, 59
Wikipedia, 47
William Safire, 103
Wine, 28, 40, 49, 63, 67, 69, 74, 77, 105
Wings, 25
Women, 4, 44, 91
Wonky, 55
Wood, 13
Wooden, 82
Woolf, Virginia, 4
Worcestershire, 55, 77, 108
Wrap, 20, 39, 55, 91
WTF, 73

Y

Yeast, 118, 123
Yellow, 35, 59, 112
Yogi, 70

Z

Zest, 88
Zone, 69

The creepy old guy who writes this stuff

In addition to being a self-taught cook with a slightly off-bubble view of the culinary experience, Dr. Maddog, a.k.a. Mark Donnelly Ph.D., is an artist, an educator, a passionate community activist, and a proud husband and father.

Dr. Donnelly is the author and photographer of several books including: **Celebrating Buffalo's Waterfront, Frozen Assets: The Beautiful Truth About Western New York's Fourth Season, The Fine Art of Capturing Buffalo, Statuesque Buffalo**, and a series of children's books.

Mark's other cookbook, **Goose the Cook**, is every bit as wacky as this one.

CPSIA information can be obtained
at www.ICGtesting.com
Printed in the USA
BVHW020502200422
634748BV00003B/29